Poverty and Perception in Jamaica

Poverty and Perception in Jamaica

A Comparative Analysis of Jamaican Households

Warren A. Benfield

University of the West Indies Press

Jamaica • Barbados • Trinidad and Tobago

University of the West Indies Press
7A Gibraltar Hall Road   Mona
Kingston 7   Jamaica
www.uwipress.com

CATALOGUING-IN-PUBLICATION DATA

Benfield, Warren A.
Poverty and perception in Jamaica: a comparative analysis of Jamaican
households / Warren A. Benfield.

p. cm.

Includes bibliographical references.

ISBN: 978-976-640-230-3

1. Poverty – Jamaica. 2. Quality of life – Jamaica. 3. Poor – Jamaica.
4. Jamaica – Economic conditions. I. Title.

HC154.Z4P6244 2010   338.97292

Cover design by Robert Harris.

Printed in the United States of America.

Contents

Illustrations

Figures

Tables

Preface

This book explains the difference between objective and subjective approaches to poverty measurement using data from the 1993, 1997 and 1999 Jamaica Survey of Living Conditions. The results suggest that there are differences between the headcount index based on the objective approach and the number of households self-classified as poor. However, this difference is largely eliminated when the definition of subjective poor is based on a threshold set at the mean consumption of households self-classified as poor. Nonetheless, there are differences in the reasons for households classifying themselves as poor and the determinants of objectively defined poverty. The explanations seem to rest on perception of vulnerability, adaptive expectations, educational attainment, labour market experiences, region or area of residence, industry and sector of employment, and involvement of children and the elderly in the labour market.

The results also point to a paradox of wealth and vulnerability which highlights that single-female-headed households are more likely to "incorrectly" classify themselves as poor, though their average level of consumption expenditure is above that of other households. This is due to the multiple sources from which single-female-headed households derive their income with significant reliance on friends and family for financial support. As a result, while their average consumption is higher, the well-being of single-female-headed households is also more vulnerable to economic and social shocks. On the other hand, objectively poor single-female-headed households who receive a larger share of their consumption from remittances and reside in homes with four or more rooms are more likely to classify themselves as non-poor and have the lowest rate of participation in social safety net programmes. Clearly, efforts to target objectively poor female-headed households are likely to lead to large targeting errors since single-female-headed households who have classified themselves as poor may seek to register and participate in such programmes.

Acknowledgements

The motivation for writing this book dates back to my work in the Policy Development Unit in the Planning Institute of Jamaica. Our constant debates and efforts to understand and better the lives of Caribbean people awakened my desire to conduct further research.

The data for this book came from five communities and the nationally representative sample survey. I am greatly indebted to members of the five communities in which I conducted qualitative interviews and well-being rankings. Their candour and helpfulness allowed me to gain unlimited access to their community and to experience very closely the essentials to their well-being. I thank the Statistical Institute of Jamaica and the Planning Institute for allowing me access and use of the Jamaica Survey of Living Conditions data and the Jamaica Labour Force Survey data sets.

This book is dedicated to my mother who fathered me, my wife and to the joy of our lives, our children: son, Warren, and daughter, Raven-Tiffany, whom we love very much.

Abbreviations

CXC	Caribbean Examination Council
GCE	General Certificate of Examination
GDP	gross domestic product
JSLC	Jamaica Survey of Living Conditions
KMA	Kingston Metropolitan Area
PATH	Programme of Advancement through Health and Education
PIOJ	Planning Institute of Jamaica
STATIN	Statistical Institute of Jamaica

Introduction

The object of this book is to explain the difference between objective and subjective approaches to poverty measurement. A number of reasons households may classify themselves as poor were identified and the need for a consistent subjective threshold was made apparent. The results show that subjective thresholds, based on the mean consumption of households self-classified as poor, accord quite closely with the objective approach. There are, however, noticeable differences in the determinants of poverty and the reasons households classify themselves as poor. One cannot conclude, therefore, that given the cost of surveys and targeting, it may be better to use the subjective approach. The subjective approach indicates other non-income dimensions of poverty or vulnerability, which are important and not captured by the objective approach. The differences identified in the book are substantial, and the issue should therefore not be choosing either one approach or the other, but rather both, choosing an approach that complements each other, as suggested by Carvalho and White (1997) and White (2002).

Households may classify themselves as poor or not poor for various reasons and, as indicated, there are likely to be inconsistencies among those households who have identified themselves as poor. It was, therefore, necessary to establish a subjective threshold that is consistent. Chapter 3 establishes subjective poverty thresholds and contrasts these with the objective poverty lines. The results suggest that asking households if they are poor and setting the threshold at the mean consumption may lead to headcounts that are comparable with the objective approach. In fact, it is striking how closely the two results compared. Poverty thresholds based on minimum survival requirements proved to be unusable. This also points to the fact that what constitutes poverty goes beyond the attainment of minimum survival requirements. It stands to reason, then, that in order to generate meaningful subjective thresholds and appropriate comparison with the objective income poverty line, care must be exercised in the wording and sequencing of the questions. Comparison of the objective and subjective thresholds made it possible to establish how far absolute poverty accords with the perceptions of what constitutes poverty in society (Ravallion 1992, 35).

Chapter 4 uses an ordered probit framework to predict households self-classified as subjective poor and contrasts these results with the objective poor, thus laying the foundation for the analysis in subsequent chapters. It was demonstrated that even in cases where different methods estimate the same level of the headcount ratio, there are still differences in the households that each method identified as poor. The results point to the likelihood of objective poor households classifying themselves as not poor, and the converse is also true. The contrasts are largely due to the underlying differences in the methodologies. While the objective method establishes a minimum standard that is based largely on nutritional attainment and other non-food essentials, it pays little or no attention to utility. The decision to classify the household as poor is informed not just by current levels of consumption, but also by the quality of social and community amenities, with no obvious account taken of the attainment of the nutritional standards. It is therefore possible that a household whose consumption is above the objective income poverty line, may not spend enough on food as may be the case for those households who suggested that their food consumption was less than adequate. In such cases, the household may classify itself as poor even if it could have spent enough on food by not spending on non-essential goods. In like manner, a household may deliberately suppress consumption in order to accumulate but, based on the objective threshold, is classified as poor, quite the opposite of the household's own perception of its well-being.

It has also been shown that the reference point for community members in terms of well-being was not based on consumption relative to that of other community members but, rather, the state of living conditions within the community relative to non-community members. The ranking of well-being made on behalf of households themselves contrasted with the community participatory ranking of households by community members, in which case greater emphasis was placed on the relative well-being within the community. This situation results in the difference in the headcount reported for the household well-being ranking and community ranking of the same households. It was also established that households residing in rural areas furthest from major commercial centres were more likely to classify themselves as poor.

There is great similarity in the factors that influence the level of consumption of households self-classified as poor and the pooled sample of all households, but there are notable differences. The extent of difference in the correlates of consumption is even greater between the subjective and objective poor. In chapter 5, it is shown that for both the pooled sample and subjectively poor, male-headed households consume significantly more than female-headed households. This result is consistent with the literature that identifies female-headed households as a disadvantaged group and a policy concern. However, female-headed households are not a homogeneous group and some households fare better than others. Here, the results show that for subjectively poor households, single-female-headed household, on average, consumed more than other households, yet they are more likely to classify themselves as poor. The use of gender of household head may therefore be a weak indicator for targeting the poor as established in this book and is consistent with Ravallion's (1996, 199) argument that "variations between socio-economic groups may be dwarfed by differences within such groups".

The results in chapter 6 also show that while male-headed households consume significantly more than female-headed households, they are also more likely to classify themselves as poor once the influence of objectively poor households is controlled for. The perception on behalf of these male-headed households of their own well-being is informed by lower educational and academic outcomes of their heads, relative to other households heads, which is also translated into lower levels of consumption. It will be shown that single-female-headed households self-classified as poor have higher than average levels of educational achievement and are even more likely than male-headed households to classify themselves as poor. The decision of single-female-headed households to classify themselves as poor seems to be motivated by the occupational and sector of employment choices or opportunities, relatively lower rates of women's labour market participation, lower-than-expected returns for women's educational achievement, the predominance of women in low-paying jobs and generally lower rates of pay for women, as suggested, among others, by Hotchkiss and Moore (1996). It is likely that gender differences in wages also reflect different career paths taken by men and women, where men tend to have more labour market work experience and longer job tenure than women. Over time, as women continue to take advantage of educational opportunities, they will gradually move into more prestigious jobs, and the results established for female-headed households will not withstand the test of time. This position is, however, tempered by the continued predominance of males in the pure and applied sciences. Some of the factors influencing the sense of well-being for households can also be addressed by public policy, but there are psychological and personality trait factors that may continue to cause some households to classify themselves as poor even if their absolute well-being were to be improved.

The results also pointed to the greater likelihood of children, in households that have classified themselves as poor, to be involved in child labour. This fact is reflected in their lower-than-average days of school attendance. The influence of the child dependency ratio on the probability of being objectively poor is consistent with expectations and the literature, but the results also suggest that an increase in the child dependency ratio increases the likelihood of being subjectively poor. The explanation offered points to the fact that children in these households may be involved in child labour and that boys as well as first-born children are more likely to be involved in this practice. The fact that single-female-headed households are more likely to classify themselves as poor and boys stand a greater chance of being involved in child labour is somewhat consistent with the literature that suggests that a mother's education has a larger effect on a daughter's than on a son's education. The result also reflects the fact that girls may be more involved in housework, and their returning to education may be greater, assuming no difference in cost (Pal 2004, 6).

Unlike the case of the child dependency ratio, the elderly dependency ratio points to reduced probability of being objectively poor, but the results are not at all times consistent, possibly indicating that the contribution of the elderly in poor households may not be always greater than their claims on the household's resources. It stands to reason that the relationship between children and the elderly in these households may be influenced by the demographic shift in the population. For subjectively poor households, however, an increase in the elderly dependency ratio suggests that these households may be more likely to classify themselves as poor. Viewed together, the elderly and child dependency ratios suggest that these households may be caught in a low-level consumption trap. However, while elderly members of objectively poor households are remaining longer in the labour market and supporting the younger generation, subjectively poor households expose their children to the labour market. There are mixed responses to the practice of child labour, and further research that addresses the long-term consequences of child labour on the well-being of households and children is needed. However, to address the immediate problem, a number of policies need to be pursued simultaneously:

1. An increase in the number of available places, especially at the secondary school level.
2. Restructuring of teaching activities, especially in communities where Friday market days are the reason for absence from school, so that academic instruction is confined to Monday through Thursday, with Fridays designated for non-academic activities. This initiative has been implemented in some schools, but it needs to be adopted in all the affected regions.
3. Children and parents should be educated about the importance of their investment in education. The benefit from this initiative may go beyond the possible gains from the existing School Lunch Programme and the Programme of Advancement Through Health and Education (PATH). The success of these programmes in increasing levels of attendance also necessitates a change from a focus on children to a broader focus on the needs of the household, recognizing that the level of school attendance is greatly influenced by parental decision to send children to school. The success of an initiative like this will also be affected by the ability of high school graduates to find jobs.

An increase in household size also increased the probability of being objectively poor as well as the likelihood of households classifying themselves as poor. This implies that policies resulting in smaller household size or reduced levels of dependence are consistent with the reduced likelihood of being objectively poor and this therefore improves a household's perceived well-being. Education of women, taking into account culture, may be the most effective means through which this policy is implemented.

This would be in addition to the biological regulation of fertility through contraceptive use, as well as the social regulation of family size and composition through fostering. All of these factors must be considered along with their concomitant influences on child-rearing and associated expenses. The household in Jamaica cannot be seen in the context of the classical notion of the household composed as a nuclear family: suppliers of labour and consumers of commodities. One may extend M.G. Smith's (1962) notion of the household to include household firms. This is in keeping with Desgupta's (1996) notion of a peasant household and Schultz's (1989, 3) argument that in the early stages of the development process the family and simple firm blend together. Household size and composition may therefore reflect coping strategies evident in the different relationships of the child (or children) to the household head. As a result, further research that analyses the livelihood strategies of households is needed.

Households who foster children and reside in urban areas are less likely to be poor. The result for the subjective poor is not consistent, pointing to increased likelihood that these households classified themselves as poor in 1999 and 1997, and a reverse of the tendency in 1993. These results are not inconsistent with the literature that child transfer tends to be from low-status to high-status caretakers, and this reflects the reality in urban areas. The latter result may be informed by the relatively better level of social and infrastructure provisioning in urban areas and the household's immediate social and physical environment. However, urban households may be exposed to greater levels of inequality and may require more resources to attain the socially acceptable minimum well-being level. It is likely that these households will continue to perceive their well-being as lower than it actually is. The instability of the effect of fostering on household perception of well-being suggests the need for further research that looks at the context within which fostering is carried out, the pull and push factors that motivate it (Castle 1995, 679), and how fostering is influenced by altruism within the extended family as well as intergenerational transfers. This may also provide insights into how the family coordinates and pools economic resources, leading to better models that reflect the conditions that constrain family choices in Jamaica.

Chapter 7 analyses the reasons households "incorrectly" classified themselves as poor. Unlike male-headed households, single-female-headed households are more likely to incorrectly classify themselves as poor. The likelihood of single-female-headed households to incorrectly classify themselves as poor is related to their higher than average educational outcomes, which also resulted in expectations that a higher level well-being will be attained. It is suggested that the divergence between their actual and expected well-being – frustrated aspirations – may have influenced these households to incorrectly classify themselves as poor. In addition to the area of residence and sector of employment, single-female-headed households' decision to incorrectly classify themselves as poor is also motivated by the level of financial support received from friends and relatives living in Jamaica and abroad. A larger proportion of these households received money as child support. It has also been shown that while the proportion of households receiving remittances is, generally, highest among those incorrectly classified as not poor, this is not significantly different from the proportion of single-female-headed households who have incorrectly classified themselves as poor. This therefore prompted an examination of the contribution of this benefit to the actual household consumption expenditure, which, not surprisingly, shows that the contribution of remittances is largest for single-female-headed households incorrectly classified as not poor. To the extent that remittances are a relatively stable source of income and the (nominal) value increases with the continuous depreciation of the Jamaican dollar, these households may perceive their well-being as better than it actually is, thereby incorrectly classifying themselves as not poor. These households were also likely to live in households with a larger-than-average number of rooms and have a lower rate of participation in social programmes. It was not possible, however, to establish whether the lower rate of participation in social programmes is based on choice or public policy.

The fact that single-female-headed households have a higher-than-average level of consumption is not based on their labour market involvement, but rather on their higher reliance on social programmes, receipt of remittances and other forms of family support. This makes them much more vulnerable to economic and social shocks. It seems therefore that the underlying factors that lead to the formation of single-female-headed households may not be consistent with the literature (Schultz 1989, 21), which suggests that an increase in the proportion of single-female-headed households is generally evident when women earn as much as men, resulting in an erosion of the economic advantage of marriage. Further research is clearly needed to establish reasons some females choose to remain single and how this relates to their perception of their own well-being. Their decision to incorrectly classify themselves as poor may be related to their greater sense of vulnerability and the involvement of their children in the labour market, possibly in petty informal trading activities where earnings are likely to be intermittent and unstable. Similarly, households whose elderly members are net users of their resources are more likely to incorrectly classify themselves as poor. Households were more likely to "correctly" classify themselves as poor as the proportion of unemployed adults increased, the principal earner was employed in the agricultural sector or their housing conditions were generally poor.

The latter result is consistent with the indicators that perform best in terms of their type I and type II errors in targeting the poor (Benfield 2007). The literature shows that *housing conditions and ownership of consumer durable* variables performed best in targeting the poor. For some households, targeting is certainly a second best remedy for poverty reduction and improved well-being. Consequently, focusing on the reasons why households are poor or classify themselves as poor may point to more fundamental policy options that may reduce or eliminate poverty rather than merely offsetting it. This argument extends the cause-based approach by recognizing that the indicators suggested or used to target households are not the underlying reasons for poverty. For instance, it may be that the discrimination experienced by women in the labour market is one of the reasons why single-female-headed households are more likely to classify themselves as poor. No amount of safety nets or insurance will improve the perception of well-being for these households. Rather, a systematic reduction and elimination of labour market distortions would. The fact that single-female-headed households are more likely to identify themselves as subjectively poor may also reflect the belief that poverty is a gendered phenomenon not captured by income or consumption (Subrahmanian 2004, 189) but rather the inequalities experienced by women – gender gaps.

Writing about the peasant's ability to emerge from poverty in Jamaica, Beckford (1999) noted that, barring emigration, the only significant scope for social mobility open to them was education. The literature, in general, supports this argument where the poor are typically seen as possessing primarily labour power to sell and, as such, policies targeted at increasing the quality of and demand for labour are typically espoused. While education clearly improves human capital, it has been shown that the returns to education may be different for men and women and also increase individual aspirations and expected well-being which, if not obtained, may leave them feeling no better off, or even feeling worse off. This somewhat differs from the literature that suggests that education, generally, raises worker productivity and earnings (Mehrotra 2000, 22). The results have implications for the earnings premium associated with different levels of education and how education contributes to the reduction of poverty or sense of well-being for households. In the case of Jamaica, school drop-out rates and the involvement of children in the labour market are seen as a direct result of the low expectation of finding a job on leaving school and, more importantly, a job that allows individuals to acquire the basic necessities. The role models are no longer teachers, nurses or policemen but rather the musical artists who may not have a school-leaving certificate. It seems, therefore, that strategies combining school attendance with various apprenticeship programmes may be more successful in keeping children (especially boys) in school. Such programmes allow children to gain labour market experience, which seems to be rewarded above their school-leaving certificate and is supported by the PIOJ (2000, 41), which points to the fact that 75.3 per cent of the fourteen to nineteen age cohort in the labour market possessed no academic certificate. Increased labour market experience may improve individual chances of finding employment, shown to influence the probability of being poor and household sense of well-being. It could also reduce the frustrated aspirations of graduates.

It is clear that the indicators suggested in this book are those directly related to the ability of the households to emerge from poverty. In addition, the reasons households classify themselves as poor relate closely with the causes and determinants of poverty: child labour, unemployment or employment in low-wage sectors, to mention a few. The dilemma faced in targeting based on these indicators is therefore obvious. The indicators suggested by households may suffer from incentive effects. One approach is to subject these households to a variety of programmes that address their vulnerability as well as poverty, but the nature of these programmes is beyond the scope of this study.

The strength of this book is in its insights into the phenomenon of poverty, using both the objective and subjective perspectives. The complementarity between these two approaches and their differences enriches our insights into the correlates and determinants of poverty and household well-being. The synergies between the approaches identified in this work are consistent with White's (2002, 513) argument that the approaches used together yield insights that are greater than the sum of the two approaches used independently. While the approach is clearly a win-win situation, greater use of participatory poverty assessment data would have been an asset. However, comparable data are not available and could not have been collected within the time frame of this research. Clearly there is need for further research that triangulates the results of objective and participatory poverty assessments, not just at the level of indicators but also in terms of consistency in the actual households identified as poor. Equally important is the need to establish the extent to which household perception of well-being is informed by movement into and out of poverty (panel data is needed). This is especially true for single-female-headed households, given their higher vulnerability. This is an area for future research.

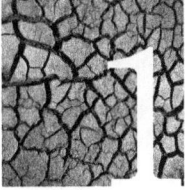

Poverty and Perception: An Introduction

Introduction

By the end of the 1990s, significant changes in the measurement and analysis of poverty had taken place in many Caribbean countries, leading to a greater understanding of its distribution across households and geographic regions. This was due in part to the parallel increase in the conduct of surveys of living conditions and the accessibility of quantitative and qualitative data on living standards and poverty. And yet, how the determinants of subjective well-being compare with the determinants of objective poverty is still today inexplicit in the Caribbean literature on poverty studies. This book fills that gap.

The principal foci of poverty research in Jamaica from the 1970s to the early 1990s were on the living conditions of the poor and the impact of the country's external debt (Ferguson 1992, 61–72) or economic adjustment on the social sector and household livelihood (Behrman and Deolaikar 1990).[1] Smith (1989) sought to understand the economic and social conditions of poverty as a basis of putting forward development plans and strategies, and Gordon (1987) highlighted the importance of considering the influence that patterns of mobility, characterized by widening inequalities, had on persistent poverty (intergenerational mobility) in Jamaica.[2] The latter showed marked consistency with Beckford's (1999) account of the experiences of peasants in the country. However, before the early 1990s, there was no agreed method of identifying or defining the poor. Subsequently, there was rapid movement towards measurement and characterization of the poor using both objective and subjective data. These two approaches pointed to discrepancies, elucidating the importance of understanding the distinction between objective and subjective approaches to poverty measurement. But no direct attempt has been made to explain the discrepancies that arise between the two approaches. This demonstrates the inadequacies of previous poverty studies. It has also resulted in gaps in our understanding of the reasons why households may classify themselves as poor, or the reasons why non-poor households, based on the objective approach, may incorrectly classify themselves as poor. As such, the formulation and implementation of poverty alleviation programmes have suffered and continue to suffer from these deficits. The multidimensional characterization of poverty suggests that the mixed methods approach is best and that any given method used to measure poverty is incapable of capturing all the facets of the condition.[3] This book seeks to better the conditions of the poor in Jamaica by filling this gap and equipping policy makers with information they need to inform social policy.

Absolute and Relative Poverty

The diverse concepts, indicators and approaches used to measure poverty reveal poverty's multidimensional nature. Poverty is experienced by individuals and households in various countries under a wide variety of conditions. Poverty is generally defined as absolute or relative and is associated with lack of income/consumption or failure to attain capabilities. It can be chronic or temporary,[4] is sometimes closely associated with inequality, and is often correlated with vulnerability, deprivation and social exclusion (Lok-Dessallien 2000).[5] The most widely used methods in developing countries tend to embrace the absolute and/or relative approaches, both of which are relevant in this book.

The concept of absolute poverty dates back to Rowntree (1901) and later Orshansky (1965). It refers to subsistence below minimum, socially acceptable living conditions usually established based on nutritional requirements and other goods deemed essential, and tends to be more applicable to developing countries. Most of the poverty studies in developing countries use absolute poverty lines. However, these studies differ in the methods used to compute poverty lines, embracing either the food energy intake method (FEIM) or the cost of basic needs approach.

Using the food energy intake method, poverty lines are set by computing the level of consumption or income at which households are expected to satisfy the normative, nutritional requirements (Foster et al. 1984; also, for elaboration, see Ravallion and Bidani 1994).[6] The other approach, the cost of basic needs method (Ravallion and Bidani 1994), adds to the cost of the nutritional, basic food basket an allowance for non-food to arrive at the poverty line. As shown in the literature and this book, these two approaches can lead to striking differences in the poverty headcount. Continuing, poverty is illustrated as a relative concept before returning to the issue of subjective poverty.

Poverty, seen as a relative concept, focuses on households at the lower segments of a population consumption/income distribution, and it is usually measured in terms of quintiles, deciles or some fraction of the mean or median.[7] There is no objective criteria for the choice of the consumption or income cut-off, and in this sense, relative measures can be seen as subjective standards of economic deprivation. Efforts to capture the relativist aspects of poverty can be traced to the contribution of Townsend (1979), with elaboration and clarification by Desai and Shah (1988), but early attempts can be found in the work of Johnson (1966). The concepts of poverty, emerging from the sociological perspective, are rooted in the underlying, structural inequalities and inherent disadvantages, resulting in the poor being unable to take advantage of assets such as credit, land, health, nutrition and education. The causal factors are related to the power structure and governance issues, as well as to the inequalities imbedded in macro-policy frameworks and distributional systems (Lok-Dessallien 2000). The human capability concept of poverty spans both the marginalist and structuralist approaches, arguing that poverty is not simply an impoverished state but also includes the lack of capabilities (Laderchi, Saith and Stewart 2003).

Several studies have attempted to modify the consumption method of defining poverty, advocating the importance of the concept of sociological deprivation. This approach expresses the importance of basic needs, as well as education, health, transport and certain social services such as sanitation. Even with such modifications, however, the definition remains largely absolutist. When considering the consumption of education, health and other commodities, along with civic rights and political power, the problem of differences in the requirements over time, and for productive social and economic engagement, is overlooked by the absolutist definition. With the Caribbean and the rest of the world undergoing rapid economic and political change, these relative aspects of poverty are certain to become relevant. This is echoed in the writings of Townsend (1979), where he observes that people are social beings who are expected to perform social roles as workers, citizens, parents, partners, neighbours and friends. Poverty should therefore be defined, according to Townsend (1979, 32), as the lack of sufficient income for people to play these roles, participate in relationships and follow customary behaviour expected of them as members of society.

It is suggested, in some parts of the literature, that relative poverty thresholds do not provide a stable benchmark against which to measure the effect of programmes and policies because they change each year in response to changes in consumption. Although there may be some truth to this argument, in the short run, it is important to note that relative poverty thresholds are not very different from absolute thresholds that rely on nutritional and non-food standards based on the judgements of technocrats. Since these may change with time, there is a degree of subjectivity in the determination of both the basic food and non-food requirements. However, while an objective poverty line may be defined and the poverty trend observed over some period, by definition there is no trend if the poor are defined using a relative standard. The next section presents the concept and methods used to derive subjective poverty.

Subjective Poverty

Applied mainly in developed countries, subjective poverty thresholds are derived by asking respondents to specify a minimum necessary income or to evaluate various income levels.[8] Minimum Income Questions, or the adequacy of consumption in relation to a number of basic needs commodities, have also been asked in surveys conducted in developing countries.

Responses to these questions tend to be sensitive to the wording of the questions and the particular method used in their derivation – even the sequencing of the questions may be important. Despite these problems, they provide information that can shed light on the extent to which objective thresholds are in agreement with individual perception of well-being, while the gap or difference – as established in this book – points to underlying differences between poverty and vulnerability.

Self-reported well-being is thought to be influenced by at least four factors, namely circumstances, aspirations, comparisons with others and personality traits or disposition (Frijters et al. 2004; Ravallion and Lokshin 2000; Lokshin and Ravallion 2002). The decision of a household to classify itself as subjectively poor is sensitive not just to the household head's personality, or the household's current level of consumption, but also its consumption relative to that of other households. This means growth that is distribution neutral may not be associated with a rising sense of well-being. In fact, Ravallion and Lokshin (2000) show that growth in gross domestic product (GDP) per capita in the Philippines is associated with a rise in the proportion of the population saying they are poor, and suggest, in keeping with the literature, that higher levels of income lead to higher aspirations and altered comparisons. Di Tella, MacCulloch and Oswald (2003) also show that contemporaneous well-being and GDP are strongly correlated as are reported well-being and growth in GDP. If income changes, the level of perceived well-being changes, such that if everyone's income falls, perceived well-being goes down.[9] This relationship between income and perceived well-being is not, however, addressed in this book.

The literature also suggests that unemployment, independent of its income effect, leads to a significant decline in well-being. This stylized fact is validated across countries, time periods and data sources. According to Frijters et al. (2004), the psychological cost of unemployment tends to be higher for men than women and greatest for young workers. Theodossiou (1998, 94) argues that joblessness leads to a marked rise in anxiety and depression, with an associated loss of confidence and self-esteem, and this is supported by other researchers (Di Tella, MacCulloch and Oswald 2003). It is also documented that marriage leads to a welfare gain over being single, while the welfare gains of having children are not conclusive.[10] These conditions influence a sense of well-being on behalf of households and their own perception of poverty status. In addition, while these studies are primarily based in developed country settings, their relevance to developing countries cannot be ignored.

The approach to subjective poverty assessment, outlined thus far, generally tends to ask individual households to respond to questions in a structured survey. In recent times, much of the subjective literature has involved the participation of several households/individuals in the assessment and ranking of well-being, much to the credit of the pioneering work of Jodha (1988) and Chambers (1994a). This has resulted in the recognition of the fact that poverty is not just about economic deprivation but about non-economic deprivation as well, leading to increased reliance on participatory poverty assessments.[11] This approach involves people in the process of defining, identifying and explaining the underlying causes of poverty and the reasons for its persistence. The participatory approach utilizes a number of methods such as mapping, time line and change analysis, seasonal calendar, and both grouping and rankings of wealth and well-being (Chambers 1994b). The latter approach was used in this research in community studies, complementing the data from the Jamaica Survey of Living Conditions (JSLC). The methods can be used flexibly, according to the situation, and contrasts sharply with other approaches where a more rigid framework and methodology are involved (Laderchi, Saith and Stewart 2003). This approach has shown that different households may not share the same view of what poverty is; there is a tendency for the very poor to underestimate income needs and for almost all other types of households to overstate it (Greeley 1994).

Obviously, adopting a broader concept of poverty leads to a more complex view, as well as the need to resolve discrepancies between types of assessment.[12] For example, Robb (1999, 23), using poverty data on Armenia, shows how conflicting data are in fact complementary. Studies by Bevan and Joireman (1997) have integrated the information-rich qualitative participatory approach together with the objective quantitative assessment to arrive at a better understanding of poverty. The literature (Carvalho and White 1997; Sahn 1999) also suggests a number of ways in which quantitative and qualitative data may be combined. In this book, the interest is not in combining the data but rather in analysing both sets of data to learn what is different from objective and subjective approaches to poverty measurement.

Strengths and Weaknesses of the Objective and Subjective Approaches

Ravallion and Lokshin (1999) argue that paradoxically when economists analyse a policy's impact on well-being they typically assume that people are the best judge of their own well-being, yet they resist directly asking them if they are better off.[13] They argue that the use of a broad set of conventional socio-economic data or current household income may not reflect well people's subjective perception of their poverty.[14] It is argued that households differ in characteristics, such as size and demographic composition, which can influence their well-being in ways not evident in their behaviour as consumers and therefore not reflected totally in their consumption behaviour. One may argue that by setting a range of different objective (consumption)-based measures a range of different dimensions of poverty may be captured. Similarly, by focusing on a narrower concept of well-being (is one person poorer than another?), subjective assessment can accord better with the objective consumption poverty data. Ravallion and Lokshin (1999, 4) argue that in Russia the objective method tended to show that larger and younger families have higher incidences of poverty, contrary to the Russian perception that poverty is more acute in older and smaller families. These results do not suggest that one method is superior to the other but rather, if used together, information that leads to greater understanding of the nature and dimensions of poverty will be derived.

This book uses two completely different, yet complementary, approaches to identify the poor: the general absolutist (consumption/income) poverty line methodologies that typically use data from Living Standards Measurement Study Surveys[15] and subjective methodologies that include people's perception in the definition and identification of the poor. Though these methodologies are increasingly used to complement each other, they are different. Also, invariably there are differences in the households identified by each, suggesting that people may be poor in different ways and for different reasons, all of which can enhance the understanding of the dimensions of poverty. Although in recent times, significant research has been conducted on the subject (Castilla 2009; Quentin 2007; Van Pragg and Ferrer-i-Carbonell 2008; Carletto and Zezza 2004; Veenhoven 2004), this book broaches and attempts to deal with an issue that no other work in the Caribbean on poverty addresses in a like manner, and if used correctly, has much utility for the academic community and policy makers. More importantly, however, the poor stand to benefit the most.

Methodology

The data used in this book are derived from quantitative structured household surveys and community participatory well-being ranking. The survey data, used for the period up to 1999, were collected by the Statistical Institute of Jamaica using a nationally representative sample of households for the whole country as well as geographical areas or regions, while the 2002 survey data were collected, primarily, to complement the community well-being ranking data and were collected in the five communities in which the participatory poverty assessments were held. The questionnaire used in the community survey retained all of the questions in the national survey, except for those on consumption, and the survey also included additional questions on the well-being ranking of households. This book makes use of both sets of qualitative data, as outlined above, using both unstructured survey response/focus group discussions and participatory well-being ranking by households. It compares these with objective poverty assessment using the JSLC and community survey data.

Jamaica Survey of Living Conditions

The JSLC is part of the World Bank's general Living Standards Measurement Study surveys. The first survey was carried out in 1988, and yearly surveys followed.[16] The questionnaire is ordered based on themes with the less sensitive information collected first. Data on health, child nutrition, education, social safety net programmes, housing conditions and consumption[17] (the commodity groups are food and beverages, fuel and household supplies, housing and household expenses, durable goods, personal care, health care, clothing and footwear, transportation, education, recreation, home production, and gifts and miscellaneous[18]) are collected.[19] Apart from the last two sections, which focus on household-level data, the other sections collect data on individuals within the household, and an often debated issue is the extent to which the respondent, who may be the head, spouse or possibly some other adult, is capable of providing accurate information about the household and, more importantly, all its members. To minimize this possible source of error, interviewers may make several visits to the household to collect follow-up information or to speak to the head of household or their spouse. Other basic survey information about each individual includes their age, gender, marital status, the head's employment status and the relationship of family members to the household's head.

Representativeness

The JSLC survey has a two-stage stratified sampling design, with the first stage being the selection of enumeration districts and the second, the selection of housing units or dwellings within the strata or primary sampling units. All housing units in Jamaica are assigned to enumeration districts, and it is these enumeration districts which are used to form the primary sampling units. There are 239 primary sampling units in the Jamaica Labour Force survey, but only 78 of these were used in the 1993 JSLC survey, while all the primary sampling units were used in the 1997 and 1999 surveys. If an enumeration district contained one hundred or more dwellings, it was designated a single sampling region. Otherwise, it was combined with adjoining enumeration districts until there were at least one hundred dwellings. The sampling regions are also formed so that they were wholly contained within one of the fourteen parishes in Jamaica, contain approximately the same number of dwellings and are expected to contain households that were generally homogeneous. At the same time, purely urban, semi-urban or rural sampling regions were created. From each sampling region, two enumeration districts were selected with probability proportionate to size. Given the large number of sampling regions or strata, the selection of samples from each ensures a more even distribution of the sample across all geographical regions. Care, however, needs to be taken to account for the movements of the population, and while this is done by updating the sampling regions, no deliberate account is made of whether the same households are within each dwelling or to which dwelling a household may have moved. Each enumeration district is selected with replacement, and in rare cases when an enumeration district is selected twice, several alternatives are used to select a different set of dwellings. Once the enumeration districts have been selected, the field staff completes a list of all the dwellings by visiting each household. From this list sixteen dwellings are selected as a systematic sample with a random start. The sample dwellings for the JSLC are usually selected as a random sub-sample of the immediately preceding Jamaica Labour Force Survey, facilitating the linking of the two data sets. Thus, one-third of the Jamaica Labour Force Survey is usually covered in the JSLC except when larger samples are required. This design is consistent with households having equal probability of selection; therefore, the population density functions should approximate the normal distribution.

This position is supported by Deaton's (1997, 10) argument that "two-stage sampling is not inconsistent with each household in the population having an equal chance of selection into the sample". Deaton further argues that "if clusters are randomly selected with probability proportional to the number of households they contain, and if the same number of households is selected from each cluster", as is the case identified above, "we have a self-weighting design in which each household has the same chance of being included in the survey". The JSLC is therefore self-weighted by design but regional weights[20] are applied, and in cases when non-response rates are high, the results are weighted accordingly. In this study non-response (which occurs in specific cases of difficulty when communities may become inaccessible due to inclement weather or violence) was not a problem for any of the years studied and regional weights are applied accordingly.[21]

Community Data

This aspect of the study was undertaken during the period February to August 2002. The selection of communities was informed by the Jamaica poverty map, the Social Development Commission's report – consultations with poor communities, the need for urban-rural comparison and communities with some variance in well-being. The experience of the Social Development Commission's community development officers, who are knowledgeable about the areas, was also invaluable. In each community, several focus group meetings were held to discuss issues, problems and concerns of community members and to assess the general living conditions in the community. Data on the living conditions of the communities were also collected in community surveys.

The survey method used to select households in each community was informed by the size and convenience of data collection within the community. In large communities such as Kingston Gardens, Enfield and Gimme-Mi-Bit, households were selected using a two-stage sampling technique, where the first stage involved the random selection of a cluster (an area or street) followed by the canvassing of the entire cluster. Two clusters each were selected in Kingston Gardens and Gimme-Mi-Bit, and one cluster from Enfield. All households were then surveyed. The communities of River Head and Water Wheel are relatively small and, therefore, there was no need to draw a sample from them – in both cases, the entire community was surveyed. All the households in the community surveys were subjected to a process of wealth (well-being) ranking whereby households placed themselves into one of four possible well-being groups.

Well-Being Ranking

To inform the variables used to explain poverty, meetings were held with several community groups and individuals to understand their perceptions of the elements of well-being. The households were allocated to wealth categories based on the criteria established by the community and the community's perception of their well-being. The notion of wealth and poverty did not vary between communities, but in one community the concepts used to define the wealth categories differed. The exercise began by asking participants in community meetings to identify the different socio-economic groups within their respective communities. Generally, three well-being groups were identified: households who are (1) very poor (2) poor and (3) "affording" (by this the community meant households who were capable of providing themselves with the basic necessities). The characteristics of each group were then discussed and recorded. In a follow-up community meeting, a smaller number of participants (between four and six residents) placed all the households in one of the well-being groups identified. The results were then triangulated by discussing the general characteristics of each group with the option of changing the ranking of any given household, but this occurred only in one case. This approach was taken in preference to one that discussed the characteristics of each household in the respective groups to minimize any possibility of embarrassment that may have resulted. Each household was assigned a pile number varying between one and three, where one was assigned to the very poor and three was assigned to households classified as affording or rich. The average score for each household rounded to the nearest whole number determined the well-being group to which it was finally assigned.

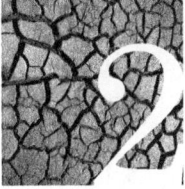

Setting the Poverty Line: An Overview

stimating poverty in Jamaica based on household Living Standards Measurement Study survey data is a recent practice, dating from 1989, with initial assistance from the World Bank. The expressed intention was to monitor the impact of economic policies geared towards transforming the economy on the poor and vulnerable. Jamaica entered its first structural adjustment programme in 1977; however, the pace of reform was significantly greater in the 1990s. The latter part of the 1980s and early 1990s saw the government embarking on trade liberalization, financial sector deregulation, privatization and labour market reforms. The initial impact of the policies was an increase in poverty over the period 1990–92, peaking at 44.6 per cent in 1991, but by 1993, the economy had rebounded and official estimates of poverty fell below their 1990 levels of 28.4 per cent. Further reductions in the poverty headcount were achieved by 1999. The literature generally attributes the initial reduction in poverty to the removal of agricultural price and exchange controls, success of the garment industry in the free trade and export processing zones, and increased inflow of remittances and net private transfers. But success in the banking and free zone sectors was short-lived. The level of decline in poverty remains a contentious issue, especially given negative or marginal real GDP growth in the latter part of the 1990s. There is dissonance between objective (16.9 per cent of individuals) and subjective

(46.1 per cent of households) estimates of the headcount reported in the 1999 JSLC, which, to the best of our knowledge, has not been reconciled. This apparent paradox between poverty headcounts and GDP growth is clarified by the data on consumption, which show that the estimates are for a period in which real per capita consumption increased from J$7,616 in 1991 to J$9,440 in 1998. There are major swings in the intervening years, and consumption falls off slightly in 1999, possibly accounting for the trend in poverty reported by the JSLC method.[1] It is quite likely that the data on consumption also picks up trends in the informal economy and remittances, which are not captured in the GDP data.

The literature pointing to growth in the Jamaican economy invariably overlooks the average GDP growth of 0.9 per cent during the 1990s, as reported by the *Economic and Social Survey of Jamaica* (PIOJ 2001), and refers to the period immediately after independence in which the economy experienced its strongest growth ever in real GDP, averaging 5.2 per cent over the period 1962 to 1973 according to the *Jamaica Human Development Report* (PIOJ 2000). From all accounts, the benefits of growth continue to be unequally distributed.[2] According to Boyd (1988, 11), "the share of aggregate income received by the bottom 40.0 per cent of the population declined from eight point two per cent in 1958 to seven per cent in 1971/72, while the share of the top five per cent of the population increased by six point eight percentage points to 37.0 per cent". In more recent times, the data for 1999 suggest that the bottom 40.0 per cent of the population consumes 17.2 per cent of total consumption compared to 30.0 per cent for the top decile.[3]

Despite continuous and deepening reform during the 1990s and other efforts to transform the economy, it remains fragile, undiversified, noncompetitive and heavily import–export dependent. All of this has caused low productivity and failure to return to a path of sustained growth. As a result, measures intended to improve fiscal prudence have had devastating social consequences, particularly for the vulnerable groups. In this light, coupled with more recent international efforts to cut world poverty in half by the year 2015, motivated possibly by the debate that points to the nexus between economic growth and poverty reduction (White and Anderson 2000; Dollar and Kraay 2000), renewed efforts are directed at identifying and targeting the poor, to which this book makes a contribution.

Previous Approaches and Estimates of Poverty

Objective Poverty

Poverty in Jamaica is currently computed based on the ability to attain a basic basket of food and non-food essentials. The food basket, recommended by nutrition and medical personnel from the Ministry of Health, was based on dietary surveys, to determine the representative consumption patterns of households[4] in the lowest two consumption quintiles.[5] Based on these surveys, a representative food basket was developed for the Kingston Metropolitan Area (KMA) by adjusting the baskets identified in the surveys to take into account minimum household needs for energy, calcium, protein and iron.[6] The basket was further modified to include, as far as possible, the lowest-cost food items without compromising the dietary constraints or needs.[7] Although the recommendations are based on human physiological requirements, it is clear that the judgements made in putting together the food basket meant that a great deal of subjectivity crept into the computation of the food standards in terms of the composition of the items and the prices that were appropriate. What is important is that these judgements reflected the conditions of the Jamaican society for which they were made. The objective poverty line was arrived at by adding an allowance for basic non-food expenditures, using the expenditure pattern of households in quintiles one and two to devise the food basket. Technically, this is done by scaling up the cost of the food basket by a multiplier for non-food consumption, which is the reciprocal of the average proportion of expenditure spent on food by households in quintiles one and two.[8] Scaling up the cost of the basic food basket by the multiplier allows for the provisioning of basic non-food requirements.[9] The difficulty with using the non-food standard as computed is that it is not clear what the standard relates to in terms of the actual goods and services consumed, and expenditures on non-food items are less stable compared with food expenditure. The proportion of expenditure on food (food share[10]) will decline with rising living standards (Citro and Michael 1995), suggesting that non-food consumption may become increasingly important over time, where the actual ability to purchase certain items may be important. This concern may, however, be addressed by looking at what non-food essentials households actually purchased, but this is beyond the scope of this book.

A further problem with this approach identified by Ravallion and Bidani (1994) is that it leads to higher real poverty lines in richer regions. This assumes that households in urban regions require a larger non-food budget in order to attain the same level of well-being as households in rural areas. In the context of Jamaica, this result is certainly not in keeping with reality, as non-food items tend to be more expensive in rural areas, invariably reflecting the cost of transportation. In addition, although it may appear intuitively plausible to set the poverty line based on the consumption pattern of individuals in the poorer quintiles, if their consumption pattern is indeed influenced by their socio-economic status where a large share of their consumption is on food, then the poverty line may be downward biased. An alternative to this approach, identified by Ravallion and Bidani (1994), is to set the minimum allowance for non-food items based on the spending of households just able to consume the minimum food requirements (this is called the food energy intake method). The poverty line so derived is referred to as an "upper bound line". Using this approach, if non-food prices are indeed higher in rural areas, even higher incidences of poverty could be expected in these areas.

Table 2.1 specifies the official poverty lines, the upper bound or food energy intake method, the cost of the food basket and an alternative approach used in this study. The food share for scaling up the cost of the basic food basket to establish the upper bound poverty line is based on the average food share of households whose food expenditure is within

Table 2.1   Poverty Lines (J$)

Years	1990	1991	1992	1993	1994	1995	1996	1997	1998	1999
JSLC	5,077	9,149	12,827	16,688	21,161	26,557	30,753	33,582	36,235	38,699
FEIM*	5,192	7,677	13,834	17,121	23,806	27,414	35,373	40,291	47,071	51,386
Food*	2,909	4,393	7,788	9,510	12,847	15,404	19,471	21,359	23,196	24,588
Alternative*	–	–	–	15,946	–	–	–	37,290	–	46,503

Notes: (1) *Our computation;
   (2) Weighted average of regional per-adult-equivalent poverty lines.
Source: PIOJ 1990–99.

Table 2.2   Headcount Index (Percentage of Households)

Years	1990	1991	1992	1993	1994	1995	1996	1997	1998	1999
JSLC	21.8	34.7	24.3	17.7	16.9	19.0	17.3	11.9	11.5	11.4
FEIM	29.1	32.1	36.4	25.5	27.6	28.3	31.1	26.8	28.2	26.8
Food	8.5	11.0	11.7	6.8	7.2	5.9	7.1	5.6	5.4	5.2
Alternative	–	–	–	22.7	–	–	–	24.4	–	24.1

Notes: The headcount indices reported in the table do not consider economies of scales.
Source: PIOJ 1990–99.

the interval 0.9–1.1 of the cost of the food basket, while the alternative approach uses the average food shares of households in quintiles two to four. Ravallion and Bidani (1994, 80–81) outline a number of a priori practical and theoretical considerations as to why the food energy intake method is not consistent, and one will expect that, as things get better, the poverty line will rise with a country's income, making comparison with previous states difficult.

Tables 2.1 and 2.2 (and figures 2.1 and 2.2) provide the trend in the poverty lines and headcount indices. The incidence reported for the JSLC and food poverty line suggests a general decline in the headcount during the 1990s. The headcount based on the food energy intake method is higher, and the trend is different from that established using the official JSLC method. A declining trend is less evident for the food energy intake method, which, apart from 1992, suggests a generally stable trend. Although lower than

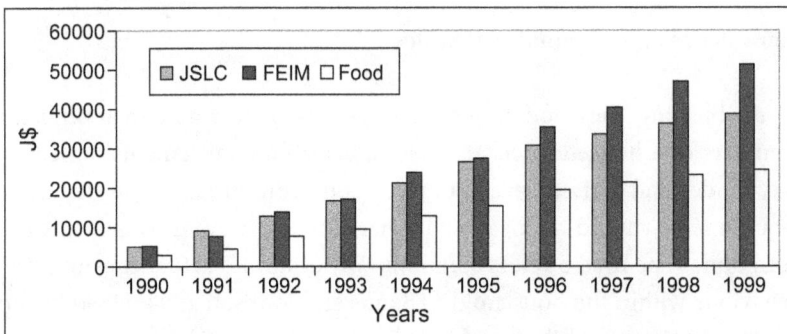

Figure 2.1   Poverty lines

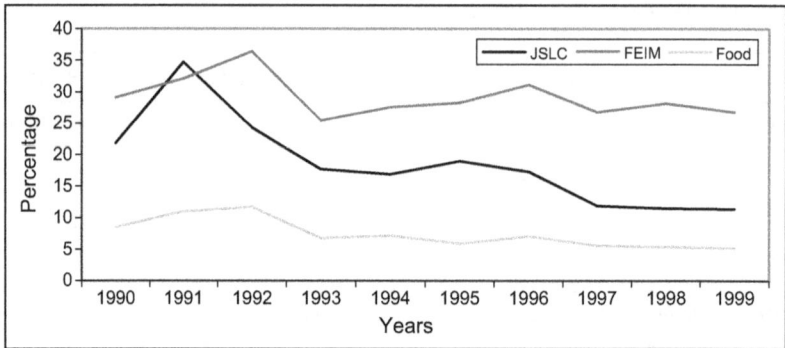

Figure 2.2   Headcount index

the food energy intake method, the same stable trend is also seen using the alternative method.

These different methods of estimating poverty are presented here to make it evident that quantification of poverty is an inexact process, which must be taken as an approximate indicator. This is evident in the different head counts generated for each method. As a result, depending on the method used, one may identify different households as poor, supporting Pyatt's (2003) argument: when the percentage of individuals who fall below the poverty line is reported, this should be read considering how the poverty line was drawn in such a way that that percentage of individuals was poor. Poverty lines are mostly useful as a means of making interpersonal comparisons of individual welfare and picking up trends over time (Pyatt 2003). From this it can be seen that objective does not imply entirely objective since there are arbitrary elements.

Equivalence and Economies of Scales

In establishing the food basket it is generally accepted that different members of a household have different calorific requirements, based on age, gender and activity level, but there is no consensus on the way these requirements should be measured. There are two ways in which this has been done. The first, but less common, way examines actual consumption behaviour within the household[11] (Banks and Johnson 1994; Haddad and Kanbur 1991a, 8), while the alternative assigns nutritional requirements based on individual characteristics and is more widely used in developing countries. Even within these two approaches, there is no consensus on the actual equivalence scale to be assigned to an individual and, consequently, quite different scales may be used to correct measures of living standards, such as income or expenditure per capita for differences in household composition.[12]

The equivalence scales used by the Caribbean Food and Nutritional Institute are generally expressed in terms of the adult male equivalence, with children and adult females requiring less than adult males. Clearly, these scales are based on food needs, and their use in constructing poverty lines implicitly assumes that non-food goods are consumed by each family member in proportion to the consumption of actual food. This assumption, however, has not been justified. The most commonly used methods of constructing equivalence scales are based on the Engel and Rothbarth procedures cited in Deaton (1997) and Banks and Johnson (1994). For both methods, equivalence scales are derived by comparing the cost associated with maintaining the same level of welfare of a particular household, both before and after a child is added to that household. The child cost is the adult equivalence expenditure for the child, but the result tends to vary with the method used. There are higher estimates with the Engel's method (Deaton 1997; Banks and Johnson 1994).[13] The use of equivalence scales to cater for the demographic composition of households generally results in expenditure per-adult equivalence that is higher than per capita, and, as illustrated by White and Masset (2003), the poverty ranking of some households may also change.

The official poverty line for Jamaica was established using equivalence scales established by the Pan American Health Organization and the World Health Organization in conjunction with the Caribbean Food and Nutritional Institute. However, in this analysis the equivalence scale assigned to all adults is adjusted to be equal to that of the adult male, given the high level of female participation in the labour market and headship, our inability to equate food and non-food needs, and the high medical costs faced by the elderly in Jamaica due to their lack of health insurance coverage.

Also of concern is the existence of economies of scale within households. There are public goods within the household, such as durable goods, shared living space, electricity and appliances. All members benefit from the use of these goods. The presence of economies of scale means that the expenditure required for maintaining a given level of welfare rises less than proportionally with household size – declining marginal cost of an additional household member. But is this rate the same for all households? And do all households have facilities at a level of quality from which it can be concluded that utility is derived? In a number of cases during the data-gathering process, households who live in shacks no bigger than sixty-four square feet (shared, in some cases, by five or more individuals) were encountered. These families have no durable assets (a noticeable few only have a radio) and their beds are made, in some instances, on a mud floor with the same clothes that are sometimes still being worn. There are also anecdotal accounts of members of poor households eating meals prepared by the household on different days and, in some homes, a cooked meal is prepared once or twice per week and members take turns sleeping because of inadequate facilities and space. All of these conditions potentially reduce the productivity of household members. It is likely that an additional member in these households may lead to further suppression of consumption. The current umbrella approach of applying a constant rate of economies of scale to all households – regardless of their assets or facilities – may, in fact, overstate the welfare of households who, in the first place, do not have the facilities or assets to share. Although these households are in the minority, the fact is that the current approach overstates their welfare (this may not move them above the poverty line, but it may affect other poverty measures) and points to the need to identify and treat these households differently, but this is beyond the scope of this book. It is expected, however, that at least economies will be had from the shared preparation of meals for the household, and the practice of sharing and handing down clothes. Therefore, conforming with the literature, per capita consumption expenditure for all households is adjusted by (C_i/AEs_i) and for economies of scale using the following equation:

$$Ce_i = \frac{C_i}{(AEs_i)^{1-\alpha}} \qquad (2.1)$$

Where (C_i) is total consumption expenditure, (AEs_i) is the sum of the household adult equivalent weights, and α is the economies of scale coefficient, which ranges between zero and one. A value of $\alpha = 0$ implies that there are no economies of scale, and the cost of maintaining the household rises proportionally with household size. This cost is, sometimes, equated with the use of per capita consumption expenditure or expenditure adjusted for household composition. On the other hand, if $\alpha = 1$, this amounts to assuming that the entire household consumption vector is a public good, and welfare is the same for different households with the same level of total expenditure, regardless of the household size.

Following this approach, different values of α within the generally accepted range of 0.15–0.3 are considered, but the reference point in all the analyses uses a value of $\alpha = 0.15$. Previous estimates of poverty in Jamaica have not considered economies of scale. These adjustments are motivated by the fact that the literature suggests that once economies of scale are taken into account, the relationship between poverty and household size disappears. In the absence of these adjustments, the poverty profile may be distorted for all population characteristics associated with household size (White and Masset 2003).

Information of relative prices is also important if credible poverty comparisons across location and time are to be derived. These comparisons inform the design of policies and provide clues necessary for more in-depth studies of poverty, its causes and its evolution. The relative rate of increase in prices by geographical regions in Jamaica is generally the same for all regions. One therefore expects that consumption patterns, in response to relative prices, are the same across regions.

There are several concepts and definitions of poverty and methods used to measure it. These methods invariably embrace some level of subjectivity and may not result in the same set of households being classified as poor. In addition, the assumptions underlying any poverty line or methodology invariably influence the head count index and those identified as poor. As a result, different poverty lines, or methods used to identify the poor, will lead to differences which should be reconciled. In fact, these differences can point us to some of the reasons and ways in which households are poor, and so aid targeting efforts and allow issues of stigma and pride to be addressed (Atkinson 1995; Besley and Kanbur 1993; Lundberg and Diskin 1995).

Having established a poverty line, the next concern is how it is updated over time. The official Jamaica poverty line is adjusted annually by the point-to-point regional consumer price indices. The approach of adjusting the original poverty threshold for inflation produces a different threshold to adjusting the poverty threshold as food costs times the food share multiplier, since changes in consumption patterns are likely to increase the multiplier. These are all judgements that have to be made, and one cannot tell which method produces a greater level of accuracy at any given point in time. However, the latter procedure may produce estimates, over time, that are more plausible. This is to be expected since using food prices, rather than just the consumer price index, is almost certainly better.

Subjective Poverty

As with the objective approach, subjective poverty also makes interpersonal comparisons of welfare, but these are based on how households perceive their well-being within society and the nature of their economic and social relations with others. However, few studies have been done using subjective perceptions of well-being in developing countries, and the ones that have been undertaken are one-shot studies, as in the Pradhan and Ravallion (2000) study on Jamaica and Nepal. The authors set out to establish subjective poverty lines based on perceived consumption needs, at the same time avoiding the approach of the minimum income question. Pradhan and Ravallion argue that since income is not a well-defined concept in developing countries, the minimum income question may not result in reliable estimates of subjective poverty. The authors constructed two subjective poverty thresholds based on perceived adequacy by households of their current level of expenditure on food alone, and their perceived adequacy of food and other non-food consumption expenditures. Households indicated whether their consumption of the commodities was "less than adequate", "just adequate" or "more than adequate" for their family needs. These responses were regressed on log total household consumption and cluster mean consumption; fraction of male and female children below eighteen years, fraction of women between the ages of eighteen and sixty years, and fraction of men and women who were older than sixty years; and regional variables for other towns and rural areas. The authors generated headcount indices for Jamaica based on households' perceived adequacy of their consumption expenditure in 1993. Three methods were used to establish subjective poverty lines, but the one of most interest to the authors and used in this book is the subject threshold based on perceived adequacy of food consumption alone. This method is of interest because it corresponds to the widely used method of constructing objective poverty lines where the level of expenditure on food is perceived as that which is sufficient to assure food consumption is nutritionally adequate for good health and normal activity levels.

Their poverty estimates varied between 34.4 per cent and 31.5 per cent and can be compared with the 31.5 per cent figure derived by the official objective method for 1993. The headcount index, derived from the perceived adequacy of food alone, compares most favourably with the objective estimates and was seen by the authors as a "more natural analogue of the idea of the subjective poverty line" (Pradhan and Ravallion 2000, 465). What was not established by the authors is the extent to which the same set of individuals or households are counted when the incidences across methods are compared, which is of concern in this book. Building on the work of these authors, it is possible not only to predict the head count indices based on subjective questions and compare these with objective estimates, but to compare the results of community participatory and objective estimates of the head count. The results from these comparisons show the extent to which the different approaches identify the same households as poor. This will also be discussed in chapters 3 and 4.

The analysis thus far has looked at two completely different, yet complementary, approaches used to identify the poor. There are the absolutist poverty line methodologies where the indicators used to identify the poor are limited to quantifiable variables and data collected in surveys (see appendix 1). Subjective methodologies include people's perceptions in the definition and identification of the poor. This approach will be shown to unearth a number of variables that are important in defining and identifying the poor and vulnerable. The objective approach cannot pick up some of these nuances. Although these methodologies are increasingly used to complement each other, they are different, and there are differences in the households identified by each, suggesting that people may be poor in different ways and for different reasons, all of which can enhance the understanding of the dimensions of poverty.

Subjective Poverty Thresholds

This chapter explores households' self-assessment of their well-being (canvassed in the 1999 JSLC [PIOJ/STATIN 2000]), examining the possibility of using two different approaches to establishing subjective poverty thresholds: (1) indirectly, by asking households how much income they need in order to survive and (2) directly, "Are you poor?" (The exact question and possible responses are shown in chapter 4.)[1] The approach relies on prevailing opinion to set the poverty threshold. The results suggest that asking households directly if they are poor may lead to more meaningful thresholds and headcount indices rather than using the minimum survival requirements. The motivation is a reality check on the levels of poverty estimates using the objective data. But, one of the subjective poverty measures does not seem realistic and in this case, it is not possible to make this reality check. The results reveal regional differences and imply scale economies and the importance of the question's wording when measuring subjective poverty.

To place this chapter in context, a brief recapitulation of the literature is provided. The literature from developing countries on poverty has primarily focused on basic needs and well-being within the context of nutritional requirements and other needs for an active life. Few studies have sought individual perceptions of well-being or socio-economic status and constructed subjective thresholds (Ravallion 1998). The literature on subjective well-being generally recognizes that one's well-being is influenced by various factors, such as household income relative to others within some reference group (such as neighbourhood or community) regardless of the level of income the household commands (Ravallion and Lokshin 2000; Ravallion 1998, 21). It is also recognized by Ravallion and Lokshin (2000) that subjective well-being varies directly with one's own income and inversely to the average income of others. Subjective thresholds are, generally, analysed from household responses to Minimum Income Questions, their account of their happiness or satisfaction and/or their own classification of their well-being at one of several possible levels (Ravallion and Lokshin 2000, 2–3; Pradhan and Ravallion 2000, 462). This chapter investigates household responses to the minimum survival requirements questions and households' self-classification of their poverty status, separately and together, as a means of establishing subjective poverty thresholds. The results are then compared with the objective poverty line. Starting with an investigation of several possible approaches, the subjective threshold is set before embracing an approach. The results, and how they should be understood, are then analysed and, finally, possible uses for subjective poverty thresholds are suggested before drawing any conclusions.

Setting the Threshold

The 1999 JSLC, unlike the others, included a number of subjective questions used first to generate subjective thresholds and assess whether or not a household is subjectively poor. The annual average consumer price indices for the period are then used to deflate the 1999 estimates and so generate subjective thresholds for 1997 and 1993. The results are contrasted with the objective poverty lines.

Minimum Survival Requirements

The first set of questions is examined to establish a subjective threshold based on households survival needs. The minimum survival requirements questions were asked in two different ways. First, households were asked,

"What is the minimum weekly amount of money you consider necessary for the survival of you and your family?" The second question: "What is the minimum monthly amount of money you consider necessary for a poor person to survive?" The response to these questions revealed, surprisingly, low weekly estimates of an average of J$49.2 (approximately J$196.8 or US$5.0 per month) for a family, with a maximum of J$1,000.0 or US$25.5 (approximately J$4,000.0 or US$102.0 per month). On the other hand, the average monthly minimum amount of money needed by a poor person to survive was J$126.0 or US$3.2 with a maximum of J$10,000.0 or US$255.1. Given the fact that the questions, both preceding and following the minimum survival question relating to the family, each asked for information relating to an individual, the response to the minimum survival requirements of the family were treated as relating to one individual. This is still very low and consistent with the fact that the response to predicted minimum survival needs (addressing measurement errors that may have occurred in its calculations) based on the log of total consumption, log household size, and gender and age of household head shows that the mean response of single-member households through to eight members, varied by at most four percentage points (see appendix 2). This reinforces the position that households were, primarily, specifying the needs of an individual.

Next, whether the average of the responses to the two questions may be used to arrive at a poverty threshold is investigated. Two possibilities are examined. The first possibility defined the poor as everyone whose actual consumption is less than the regional maximum amounts given in response to the two questions, since the means were ludicrously low. The results are J$29,000, J$8,200 and J$15,400 for KMA, other towns and rural areas,[2] respectively, and result in, counterintuitively, low estimates of 2 per cent of households being poor. The maximum minimum survival requirements in the KMA is comparable to the per-adult equivalent nutritional low-cost food basket or food poverty line. This supports the notion that individuals were primarily referring to food needs in their responses to the questions outlined above. At the same time, the maximum minimum survival requirements in other towns and rural areas were 67.6 per cent and 39.1 per cent below the minimum nutritional food requirements. Following a number of adjustments outlined below, the threshold was set at the mean minimum survival requirements of households satisfied with life.

Subjective Poor

Second, classifying the poor as all households whose per-adult equivalent consumption expenditure is below the maximum total expenditure of those who have identified themselves as poor produces an absurd estimate of approximately 100 per cent of Jamaicans as poor. The same result obtains for 1997 and 1993 in relation to households who classified their income and food consumption as less than adequate. Understandably, one may be tempted to define the poor as those households who have identified themselves as falling into this socio-economic group. This will certainly lead to inconsistency in the resulting poverty measures since people with the same level of consumption will be regarded and treated differently. It is therefore necessary to allow for heterogeneity (relativity and non-income dimensions) such that people with the same level of consumption are considered equally poor for consistency, though they may regard their well-being differently. In this light, a threshold that is not only simple and transparent but also plausible is required.

In relation to poverty lines, consistency refers to the ranking of households as poor. The poverty ranking of households will be consistent if the distribution of consumption remains constant over time or if households along a given consumption distribution are classified such that all households below a given threshold or point on the consumption distribution are classified as poor, in spite of the fact that some households below the threshold may not see themselves as poor. Consistency requires that the poverty threshold be fixed in terms of the level of well-being implied (this can be the mean, median or maximum, but as shown, the maximum may not lead to intuitively plausible results).

If the threshold is set at the mean consumption of households self-classified as poor – adjusted for household composition and economies of scales – the respective headcounts for households predicted within these groups are 24.3 per cent, 37.3 per cent and 14.2 per cent for 1999, 1997 and 1993. This result may be criticized on the grounds that the standard is based on the consumption of households self-classified as poor. But the results based on households whose income or food consumption is adequate are not intuitively plausible, with over two-thirds of households below the mean. The estimates of poverty based on households' average consumption, that of 24.3 per cent or 26.3 per cent for 1999 (see table 3.1),

Table 3.1   Subjective Thresholds

Area	1999	1997	1993
Minimum Survival Requirements			
KMA	18,256	15,627	6,907
Other towns	10,601	9,383	4,211
Rural areas	7,138	6,050	2,708
Jamaica	10,949	9,395	4,182
Headcount $\alpha = 0.15$	0.40	0.40	0.60
Headcount $\alpha = 0$	0.60	0.50	0.90
Adult Equivalent Per Capita Consumption			
KMA	54,061	46,275	20,454
Other towns	51,170	45,289	20,325
Rural areas	45,813	38,832	17,384
Jamaica	49,139	42,124	18,792
Headcount $\alpha = 0.15$	24.30	27.70	29.30
Headcount $\alpha = 0$	26.30	29.90	31.00
Poverty gap	29.90	29.90	31.60
Scale Factors			
KMA	1.13	1.19	1.25
Other towns	1.04	1.18	1.22
Rural areas	1.02	1.07	1.12
Jamaica	1.06	1.13	1.18

Notes: (1) The regional average annual consumer price indices for all commodity groups were used to adjust the 1999 estimates for other years; (2) The estimates for Jamaica are weighted.

Source: PIOJ various years.

are not significantly different from the objective estimates reported in table 2.2. This clearly supports the notion of simply asking households if they are poor and setting the poverty threshold at the mean consumption of households predicted as poor. Similar questions were not asked in the 1997 and 1993 surveys, but estimates for these years were derived by deflating the estimates for 1999. These results compare more favourably with the objective estimates for the respective years than estimates derived based on the mean of households whose income or food consumption was inadequate. The households classified as poor for 1997 and 1993 (based on the 1999 deflated mean) may not be the same as those self-classified as poor. In fact, all of the households estimated to be subjectively poor in 1997 were also poor if the threshold was set at the mean consumption of households self-classified as poor. The result for 1993 is the opposite of that for 1997, whereby 48.6 per cent of households estimated as subjectively poor were also seen as poor if the threshold was based on the mean consumption of households self-classified as poor, but the latter group of households are all estimated as poor.

One may ask: why set the threshold at the mean consumption rather than at the maximum or median? To address this question, the results of thresholds set at the maximum and median are analysed. With the threshold set at the maximum, 71.7 per cent of households are estimated as poor, while at the median, 23.3 per cent of households are estimated as poor. The respective poverty gaps are 45.0 per cent and 28.6 per cent (see appendix 3). The estimates of the poverty line, headcount and poverty gap based on the median are less than those based on the mean (see table 3.1), suggesting that the distribution is slightly skewed to the right, but the difference in these values do not point to any cause for alarm.

Subjective Thresholds

So what are the subjective poverty thresholds? The subjective poverty thresholds for 1999 are the predicted mean minimum survival requirements of households satisfied with life and the mean per-adult equivalent consumption of households predicted as poor. A household is classified as subjectively poor if its adult equivalent consumption expenditure, adjusted for scale economies, is equal to or below the thresholds reported. There are two sets of estimates: the first, and less plausible, is based on the mean minimum survival requirements of households who are satisfied with life, and the second, the mean consumption of households classified as subjectively poor. The thresholds and headcounts for the other years are based on the 1999 thresholds deflated accordingly. The subjective thresholds and headcount indices are reported in table 3.1.

The results for minimum survival requirements must be understood within the context of people surviving or making ends meet. Survival may be seen as the borderline between life and death, and everyone who is alive or surviving may necessarily say that they need less than they actually consume in order to survive. The results show that the vast majority of households are above the mean minimum survival requirements level, and it is therefore not surprising that they suggest they need less than they actually consume in order to survive. This points to the fact that what constitutes poverty goes beyond the attainment of the absolute minimum survival requirements and it also supports Kilpatrick's (1973, 329) argument somewhat that the response of households to questions on income adequacy relative to their average household income suggests a positive elasticity less than one. Simply put, households are likely to suggest that their minimum requirements are less than their current income.

A number of alternative scenarios for setting the poverty threshold based on the minimum survival requirements are investigated. Analysis of the response to minimum survival requirements from individuals who classified themselves in the survey as poor shows that, in almost all cases, the average amount specified was less than their current level of consumption. The minimum survival requirements identified by these individuals as necessary for survival were not much different from those identified by all individuals in the sample, which is unsurprising since they are surviving. If the poverty threshold were to be based on the minimum survival requirements suggested by these households, the estimate of poor households will be less than the 2 per cent reported above.

An issue that must therefore be addressed is the extent to which the concept of income and/or expenditure derived from the survey is the concept that respondents have in mind when they answer the question on minimum survival requirements. More plausibly, it is quite likely that different households have different concepts of income, which may not correspond to the established notion of income as the maximum consumption without depleting current wealth. Some households may also perceive their current income as lower than it actually is by excluding imputed income from home production, gifts and own housing; income may be seen as synonymous with money income. In other cases, they may not know their actual income, especially if it is derived from multiple sources. An examination of home production and gifts in the 1999 data reveals that although it averages about 5 per cent, there is significant regional variability in the contribution of home production and gifts to total consumption expenditure. The maximum contribution of home production and gifts to total consumption by region shows that in the KMA, other towns and rural areas it was 42.9, 84.0 and 74.2 per cent, respectively. To what extent did this factor influence the response to survival needs?

If the response of individuals to their minimum survival requirements did not include home production and gifts, and is based only on their cash expenditures, then it is not surprising that these estimates are downwardly biased. The possibility of using the minimum survival requirements by estimating them as a function of total expenditure and cash expenditure as a share of total expenditure is examined further. If households estimated minimum survival requirements based on cash expenditure only, then the subjective poverty threshold may be derived as minimum survival requirements divided by the share of cash expenditure in total expenditure. Minimum survival requirements are regressed on the share of cash expenditure in total expenditure and total expenditure. The results suggest that a one-unit increase in the ratio of cash expenditure to total expenditure increased minimum survival requirements by J$103.1, but this coefficient, unlike total expenditure, was not significant. If respondents were primarily referring to the minimum survival requirements of an individual in their response to the questions, and per-adult equivalent total expenditure is used instead, both coefficients become significant. Even after the adjustment to account for non-cash consumption, the estimate of the mean minimum survival requirements is still clearly downward biased relative to households' current expenditure, and the regional maximum specified by all households in the sample remains unchanged.[3]

The inability to use unadjusted minimum survival requirements as an indicator of poverty may be related to the fact that the two concepts are different and households are primarily referring to food needs in their response.[4] The regression results of minimum survival requirements on the *share of expenditure on food* and *total expenditure* suggest that both variables are highly significant factors influencing the dependent variable. The latter line of argument is pursued, and the response to survival needs is scaled up to include an allowance for non-food consumption based on the current total expenditure pattern of households. Two general approaches may be pursued: either scaling up some accepted level of survival needs based on the average consumption pattern of a reference group of households or consumption expenditure of those households whose survival requirements are within some interval of what is deemed socially necessary. There is no criterion, however, on which to base the minimum survival needs, and the mean and median values are downwardly biased. Instead, the minimum survival requirements of each household were scaled up based on their own consumption pattern. The resulting mean expenditure needed to survive for the KMA, other towns and rural areas is J$7,250.4, J$4,918.5 and J$4,059.4, respectively. The estimate of minimum survival requirements is likely to be a function of total expenditure and other household characteristics. The following variables are therefore used: *adult equivalent per capita total expenditure, log household size, age, age square, marital status* of household head, and two regional dummy variables for *KMA* and *other towns* to predict minimum survival requirements. All the variables, except *other towns*, are significant. The predicted average regional minimum survival requirements are not significantly different from the estimates reported above. The results also point to non-negative values of minimum survival requirements that are intuitively very low and should be dropped. But clearly there is the problem of deciding which values are low.

In order to get around the need to make a subjective decision, the estimates are based on the mean of households who suggested that they are satisfied or are very satisfied with life. The mean predicted minimum survival requirements of households who suggested that they are satisfied with life (7.4 per cent of households)[5] are J$18,255.8, J$10,601.1 and J$7,137.7 for KMA, other towns and rural areas, respectively (seen in table 3.1), and the minimum values are J$4,534.6, J$3,618.5 and J$2,336.0, respectively (the minimum values are below the annual daily cost of one beef patty in the year 1999). None of the households satisfied with life were estimated to be objectively poor, while 1.4 per cent were predicted to be subjectively poor.

Results

What do the results show? First, the results of the minimum survival requirements are examined before turning to the second set of results. The regional thresholds suggest that minimum survival requirements in the KMA are, generally, more than twice those in rural areas and approximately one- and two-thirds of the level in other towns. The regional differences in survival requirements possibly reflect the regional disparities in development: the higher the level of inequality in urban centres, the greater the level of mobility required. Use of transportation is greater, and there is a wider use of markets. This result also suggests that income may not be a well-defined concept in rural areas, evident in higher levels of sharing of resources and property.

Further, comparison with the objective method points to the controversial issue of urban versus rural poverty comparison and supports the argument by Pradhan and Ravallion (2000, 469) that absolute methods, which tend to fix the real value of poverty lines between urban and rural sectors, may underestimate poverty in urban areas. Relative to the objective income poverty method, minimum survival requirements approaches have resulted in a rank reversal of the regional distribution of poverty, with a higher percentage of urban households classified as poor. However, the estimates based on minimum survival requirements are generally ridiculously low, varying between 0.4 per cent and 0.9 per cent for the period under review. At the maximum minimum survival requirements for households satisfied with life, just 6.3 per cent of households are below the threshold.

Estimates based on the mean consumption of households classified as subjectively poor are, generally, comparable with the objective income poverty headcounts. These results compare much more favourably, in 1997 and 1993, than estimates based on the mean consumption of households whose income and food consumption were inadequate. This is seen in the difference in scales, reported in table 3.1, between the threshold based on this method and the objective income poverty line, supporting the idea of simply asking households whether they are poor and setting the threshold at the mean.[6] Unlike the first approach, the regional poverty ranking of this approach is also consistent with the objective income poverty method. These results also suggest that the causes of deviations between subjective and objective poverty, addressed in chapter 5, are uncorrelated with consumption.

The thresholds are set at the means, but poverty lines can be derived for households of different sizes and are shown to increase – though less than

Table 3.2   Poverty Thresholds by Household Size, 1999

HH Size	Predicted Minimum Survival Requirements		Adult Equivalent Per Capita		Per Capita	Official Average Per-Adult Equivalent Weights
				Subjective Poor		
		Economies		Economies	Economies	
1	12,691.8	1.00	56,531.9	1.00	1.00	1.00
2	15,672.2	1.23	54,177.6	0.96	0.93	0.95
3	10,548.1	0.83	51,204.8	0.91	0.84	0.90
4	10,306.3	0.81	47,909.6	0.85	0.78	0.85
5	9,100.4	0.72	44,899.7	0.79	0.77	0.82

Note: Estimates based on the threshold of mean consumption of subjective poor;
    HH: household
Source: PIOJ various years.

proportionately – with household size. Thus, as household size increases, individuals are suggesting that they need, on average, less income in order to survive. As seen in table 3.2, an adult who lives in a five-member household suggests that the average minimum survival requirements she needs is 72 per cent of that of someone living alone. This result may seem inconsistent with previous arguments that households were specifying individual needs, but it may reflect possible economies of scale in the adjustments made for non-food requirements. Table 3.2 also reports a similar trend based on the mean consumption of households classified as poor. This clearly captures the effect of household size and economies of scale. The results compare with the average per-adult equivalent weights based on nutritional requirements and used in adjusting household expenditures and estimating objective income poverty.

Of what use are subjective thresholds? It is important to note that, unlike an absolute income poverty line, this approach does not consider minimum nutritional requirements for good health, the minimum needs for membership of society, enjoying a reasonable standard of living or the age or gender composition of households. It accords with the concept of basic survival needs, which is, clearly, downward biased, and an average of what households deem to constitute poverty. The results, however,

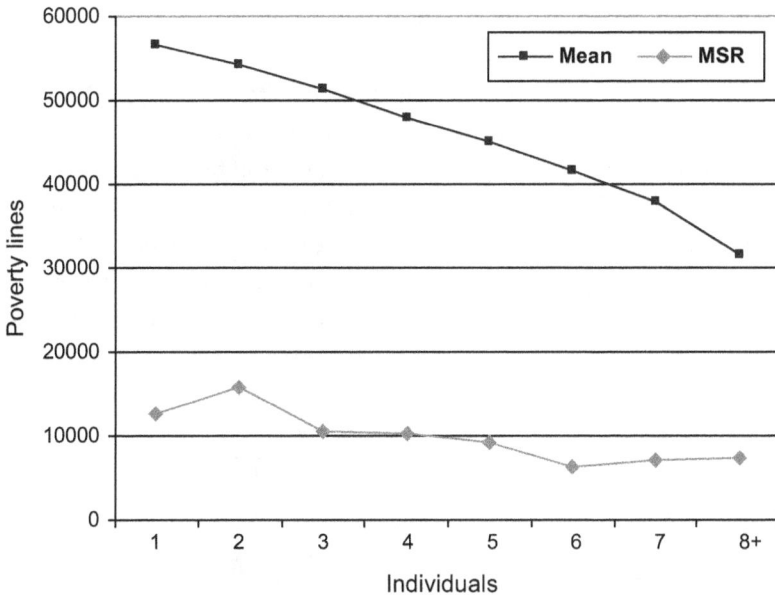

Figure 3.1   Individual poverty lines, 1999

suggest that minimum survival requirement is not appropriate as a means of judging the sufficiency of the food and non-food standards used in setting the objective poverty line. The attraction of this type of approach is that it does not require detailed data on household consumption and considers what people actually consume, incorporating household preferences and taste. This approach is, however, likely to be seen as arbitrary, since there is no objective standard analogous to the minimum nutritional requirements to which subjective thresholds are linked. Nevertheless, by the nature of the approach, the need for objective standards are not essential, but the data on minimum survival requirements, though interesting, cannot be used to establish meaningful subjective poverty thresholds. It stands to reason, then, that in order to generate meaningful subjective thresholds in the first instance, an appropriate comparison with the objective income poverty line requires a different question. The question should invite households to suggest an amount that would allow them to enjoy a reasonable and/or decent standard of living rather than an amount needed for survival. At the same time, the thresholds based on household self-assessment of their poverty status may allow for more meaningful comparison. It is indeed striking how close these estimates are to the objective headcount, particularly in 1999.

In addition to the use of subjective thresholds to judge the sufficiency of objective income poverty lines, they have also pointed to the existence of economies of scales within households. In addition, the subjective poverty thresholds for individuals within households of different sizes, as seen in figure 3.1, are shown to decrease, much more so in the case of the threshold based on mean consumption of households classified as poor than for the minimum survival requirements. The implied level of economies of scales, though small, may be used as a guide to the actual level of economies of scales that should be incorporated into the objective approach. These results suggest that prior to any comparison with the subjective approach, the objective method should incorporate economies of scales.

Conclusion

This chapter examined the use of household self-assessment of well-being to derive subjective poverty thresholds. The results of the threshold based on households' minimum survival requirements are unusable and suggest as well that attempts to arrive at meaningful subjective thresholds must pay close attention to the wording and sequencing of the questions. It is preferable to ask households to specify an amount of income that will allow them to enjoy a decent standard of living, rather than an amount for survival. This question will lead to more meaningful estimates. It is not surprising that the minimum survival requirements specified by households is, generally, less than the cost of the minimum nutritional food basket since, unlike the former, the latter considers factors such as good health, work load, age and gender, to name a few. Nonetheless, this approach has raised important issues such as the relative well-being between urban and rural regions and the geographical poverty ranking between the two.

The thresholds based on the mean consumption of households self-classified as poor accord quite closely with the objective method, with similar trends in the geographical poverty ranking. This threshold shows that the objective income poverty line accords with the general notion of what constitutes poverty in the society and also supports the adjustments made to household expenditure to account for household composition and the effects of economies of scales. It is, however, not possible to establish the robustness of the results for the subjective poor in other settings, and the results may be seen as data-specific. Because the mean has demonstrably performed relatively well over the period, the latter claim cannot be made. The next chapter looks at the second use of subjective poverty data analysing household poverty status based on households' own assessment and the extent of overlap with the objective approach.

Modelling Subjective Well-Being

T his chapter models the determinants of people seeing themselves as subjectively poor, based on responses of households to a number of subjective well-being questions in the JSLC and other community surveys. Using ordered probit models and factors, based on the literature, that tend to influence households' sense of well-being, the number of households who classified themselves as poor is predicted. The extent to which these households are the same as those estimated as objectively poor is analysed. Further, the degree to which households are poor on both fronts indicates the extent to which the approaches are substitutes and these households are defined as unanimously poor. This analysis is motivated by the fact that subjective poverty data are a good measure of well-being, and as such, systematic deviations from objective poverty inform about the determinants of well-being that are different from consumption.

The chapter is divided into five sections: the first section outlines households' ordinal ranking of their subjective well-being, followed by a section on the methodology used to model the determinants of people perceiving themselves as poor. The empirical results are then analysed, followed by an analysis of the consistency between the objective and subjective approaches and a brief conclusion.

Subjective Well-Being

As argued in chapter 2, there is an inherent subjectivity and social spe-
cificity to any notion of basic needs, poverty or well-being, and these are
ever-changing over time. Psychologists and sociologists also recognize
that the circumstances of an individual relative to others, in some reference group, influence households' perception of their well-being at any
given level of individual command over commodities. Several papers,
which have addressed the issue of subjective poverty by analysing subjective responses to minimum income questions, such as that by Stanovnik
(1992), have found that the responses tend to be an increasing function
of actual income. Nevertheless, it is also recognized that other household
characteristics, such as family size, demographic composition, geographic
neighbourhood, employment status and personality traits, also influence
households' response to questions about their well-being (Ravallion and
Lokshin 2000; Pradhan and Ravallion 2000).[1] With the exception of personality traits, the above variables have been used to predict the subjective
headcount index.

In order to evaluate households' subjective well-being, their responses to
a number of subjective questions, which require households to select one of
a set of ordered well-being levels, were used. The questions ranked various
well-being levels. In 1999, the question, "To which class does the family
belong? – (1) upper, (2) upper middle, (3) middle middle, (4) lower middle,
(5) working, (6) poor, (7) do not know" was asked of the JSLC respondents.
Next, the range of responses to the subjective questions in the 1997 and
1993 JSLC and community surveys are outlined. The 1997 question in the
JSLC survey for households was, "Concerning your household income over
the past year, which of the following is true? (1) Less than adequate (LA)
for the household's needs (2) Just adequate (JA) for the household's needs
(3) More than adequate (MA) for the household's needs." In the 1993 JSLC
survey, households were asked, "Concerning your family food consumption, housing, clothing, access to transport facilities, health care, children
schooling: (1) it was less than adequate for your family's needs? (2) it was
just adequate for your family's needs? (3) it was more than adequate for
your family's needs? (4) not applicable." For each basic needs commodity

or well-being group, the household chose one of the responses; as such the response to each item or category is mutually exclusive.

The same questions asked in the 1993 JSLC survey were duplicated in the 2002 community survey and, in addition, the households were asked, "In which wealth group do you place your household? (1) very poor, (2) poor, (3) affording, (4) rich, (5) other." Although the question in the 1993 JSLC is directly comparable with the questions asked in the community survey, the same cannot be said for the other years. Nevertheless, each question was geared to measure the well-being of households, albeit different dimensions of that well-being making for even more interesting comparison with the objective approach.

The responses to the questions on consumption adequacy and class are summarized in table 4.1. Taken at face value, the well-being scores appear to be skewed towards the lower end of the possible answer distribution, suggesting that people, on average, are just "getting by" or are poor.

The questions outlined above do not presume that income or consumption is the only variable relevant in defining the poor, but they also leave the decision up to the respondent. In addition, by wording the 1999 and 2002 survey questions in terms of poor and upper class, the questions focus on a narrower concept of well-being than questions relating to happiness, satisfaction or even adequacy of food consumption or income. The proportion of households who classified themselves as poor or having inadequate income/consumption in table 4.1 differs from the objective headcount. It does not appear, however, that discrepancies between the subjective answers and objective income poverty reflect the fact that they are measuring different things. The same argument applies to the comparisons using community data. Estimates of subjectively poor households are generated using the various types of community data, and the extent to which the methods identify the same households as subjectively poor is analysed. This also offers the possibility of analysing how different subjective meanings attached to the complex concept of poverty relate to the objective approach. This issue will be discussed at a later stage and we will now turn to the methodology used in predicting households who are subjectively poor.

From table 4.1, it is clear that the outcomes to the questions are ordered. This means that the variable of interest – the dependent variable – is both discrete and ordinal. In this case, a linear regression will treat the difference between, for example, affording and poor identically to the

Table 4.1 Distribution of Well-Being Groups

Read categories excluding 1999 & 1997	Community				1993				Community		1999		1997	
	MA	JA	LA	NA	MA	JA	LA	NA	Well-being		Class		Adequacy of income	
Food	11	56	33	–	6.3	54.6	39.1	–	Very poor	25.7	Poor	43.7	LA	56.3
Housing	11	52	37	–	7.5	50.2	42.3	0.1	Poor	45.2	Working	29.6	JA	41.6
Clothing	11	62	27	–	7.1	57.2	35.7	–	Affording	28.6	Lower middle	11.5	MA	2.1
Access to transport	13	57	30	–	4.5	47.5	47.9	0.2	Rich	0.5	Middle middle	7.8		
Health care	13	51	36	–	3.7	55.1	40.9	0.3			Upper middle	2.0		
Children's schooling	6	31	30	33	2.3	34.6	20.0	43.1			Upper	0.8		

Note: In the 1999 survey, nine households did not respond to the question on economic class while 87 households (4.7 per cent) responded that they did not know which class they belonged to. These households were not included in the ordered probit model.

Source: PIOJ various years, and community surveys.

difference between poor and very poor, whereas, in fact, the numbers are only a ranking and have no cardinal significance. Estimating the ordinal dependent variable using a multinomial logit will result in the discarding of the information conveyed by the ordered nature of the data. The appropriate method for estimating (dependent variable) models with more than two outcomes and where the variable is both discrete and ordinal is an ordered probit as used in this analysis.[2]

Methodology

Here, it is assumed that each household had its own expected consumption norms and general well-being at the time of being interviewed, and with the prevailing income and prices, there is no assumption that these needs or expectations are achieved given the household's utility maximizing consumption vector. There are N households in our sample (indexed $i = 1, \ldots, N$) and each household's well-being can be represented as T_i. The model may be specified accordingly:

$$T_i = \beta_k' X_{ik} + \varepsilon_i \tag{4.1}$$

Let T_i^* be the unobservable consumption or well-being norms of the ith household; T_i^* is a function of a number of determining factors, K, such as household and regional characteristics (influencing the probability of any of the i households belonging to a well-being group, whose value for household i are X_{ik}, $k = 1, \ldots, K$). In addition, let β_k be the vector of parameters to be estimated, and ε_i a random error term assumed to be independently and identically normally distributed. The problem with this equation is that T_i^* is a latent variable, which is unobservable either in principle or in practice, and as such the equation cannot be estimated. What is observable, however, is a household's level of consumption adequacy or class.[3] The classification of a household in terms of the adequacy of its consumption/income and class depends on the value of the latent variable in conjunction with the threshold values Z_j. Households are classified as poor if the probability of the value on their latent variable being below the threshold Z_j is greater than 0.5.[4] The probability of a household being classified as subjectively poor is given by the probability of their consumption level plus an error term being below the first cut-off point. However, the response of households to their well-being status in the community survey was more appropriately analysed using a probit model.

For each household i, any one of the J responses, for example, to Class in table 4.1 can be selected, where their choices are mutually exclusive and collectively exhaustive. Let the values taken by the observable variable J_i represent the selection of any one of the responses for household i such that $J_i = 1$ if the first option is selected by any household; $J_i = 2$ if the second option is selected, and up to the point where $T_i = J$ if the last option is selected. Here, the options are ordinal but with no implication for differences in strength of the selection. The ordinal ranking in households' responses to the adequacy of income/consumption, and well-being group or class, "allows" for the application of the ordered probit model where observed well-being:[5]

$$T_i = \begin{cases} 1 \ if -\infty \leq T_i^* \leq Z_1 \ (consumption\ LA\ or\ HH\ poor) \\ 2\ if\ Z_1 < T_i^* \leq Z_2 \ (consumption\ JA\ or\ HH\ belong\ to\ working\ class) \\ 3\ if\ Z_2 < T_i^* \leq \infty\ or\ Z_3 \ (consumption\ MA\ or\ HH\ in\ lower\ middle\ class) \\ 4\ if\ Z_3 < T_i^* \leq \infty\ (middle\ and\ upper\ classes) \end{cases}$$

and the Z_j are the thresholds to be estimated. Table 4.2 summarizes the results of the models.

Empirical Results

The variables used to predict subjective poverty are *current level of consumption, log of mean household consumption relative to the cluster mean consumption,* or *mean consumption of the electoral district* (sensitivity analysis was also done using the mean consumption of quintiles), the composition of the household instrumented by the number of *children* and *elder* members, *union status of the household head, number of rooms per person* (as an instrument of living conditions) and the *proportion of employed adults*. The *proportion of employed adults* is used instead of the employment status of the head, since the nuclear family structure is not pervasive in Jamaica and

Table 4.2 Subjective Poverty Predicted

	Community 2002				1999		1997		1993	
	Wealth Group		Adequacy of Food							
	Probit		Ord. Probit							
Robust Std. Errors	Coeff.	Std. Error	Coeff.	Std. Error	Coeff.	Std. Error	Coeff.	Std. Error	Coeff.	Std. Error
Lnaecapita	-0.198	0.183	0.496	0.250*	1.062	0.104**	0.273	0.108*	0.667	0.112**
ln hhcon/cluster	-0.000	0.000	-0.000	0.000	-5.108	1.382**	3.516	1.432*	0.296	1.332
# of children	-0.090	0.086	0.032	0.074	0.010	0.021	-0.053	0.022*	-0.061	0.021**
# of elderly	0.176	0.205	-0.259	0.168	0.091	0.051+	0.045	0.054	-0.022	0.048
Union status of head	-0.333	0.227	0.089	0.192	-0.418	0.057**	0.195	0.058**	0.061	0.060
Prop. of adults emp.	0.154	0.267	-0.117	0.226	-0.126	0.136	-0.026	0.139	-0.071	0.126
Rooms per person	-0.375	0.184*	0.264	0.153	0.152	0.036**	0.108	0.035**	0.087	0.035*
Log likelihood			-140.01		-1975.98		-1432.99		-1533.98	
# of observations	161		159		1785		2012		1951	
Joint sig. of regressors	WaldChi2(7) = 13.39 Prob>chi2 = 0.063		LR Chi2(7) = 15.74 Prob>chi2 = 0.030		LR Chi2(7) = 397.91 Prob>chi2 = 0.000		LR Chi2(7) = 234.47 Prob>chi2 = 0.000		LR Chi2(7) = 334.72 Prob>chi2 = 0.000	
Pseudo-R sq	0.070		0.053		0.092		0.076		0.098	
Cut 1 (Constant)	(3.291)	3.169	4.776	2.521	7.188	0.596	6.596	0.574	6.862	0.534
Cut 2			6.557	2.538	8.150	0.600	8.616	0.588	8.872	0.546
Cut 3					8.698	0.603				
Predicted Poor	95.0		14.0		43.5		66.7		27.4	

Note: **1 per cent level; *5.0 per cent level; +10 per cent level.

households may have several adult members living together, especially in female-headed households. In addition, it is anticipated that the *proportion of employed adults* may also capture some of the effects of changes in macroeconomic variables such as GDP.

In estimating the models, the issue of whether all the variables – even when their coefficients were not significantly different from zero – should be retained in the model was considered. A number of scenarios were investigated in which the insignificant variables were omitted, and it was found that the predicted probabilities did not change significantly in any given year but the poverty status of between twenty and thirty households did change. All of the variables were retained since there is theoretical justification for doing so in predicting households self-classified as poor.

In addition, the effect of including the log of mean consumption of the enumeration districts, instead of that of quintiles, was investigated. The results point to no significant change in the proportion of households classified as poor but, generally, an equal number of households changed status, varying between 122 in 1999 and approximately 30 in 1993. The issue here is whether the neighbourhood effect is best captured by the enumeration district *means* as opposed to that of *quintiles* or some other variable. Enumeration districts tend to cut across communities that, based on political divide, may not relate to each other, and this is particularly evident in the KMA. Added to this, the fortunes of different parts of an enumeration district may be dependent on the political party in government. More importantly, from our experience in conducting the community surveys, people's reference points seemed to extend beyond enumeration districts (not overlooking the larger variance) or communities, which generally are only important in an administrative sense and specifically in the context of general elections (notwithstanding the survey design); as such, the inclination was to use quintiles.[6] A variable that looks at the *household's consumption relative to that of the community* may be a more appropriate way of capturing the neighbourhood effect (see table 4.2). Analysis of the effect of including this variable shows that at no point has the estimated headcount changed significantly, and the number of households who changed places varied between 71 in 1999 and 11 in 1993.

The signs on the significant variables in the ordered probit models are generally positive, except for *number of children*. This suggests that for those variables that are significant, a one-unit increase, such as in *number of rooms per person*, results in a significant decline in the probability of the household classifying its consumption/income as inadequate or being in poverty, and increases the probability of the household classifying its consumption/income as more than adequate or belonging to the middle class and above. Unlike the other variables, *number of rooms per person* remained significant for the entire period and suggests that housing quality or level of congestion in the household plays an important role in the perception of well-being status. This interpretation also holds if households' mean consumption increases generally or relative to the average in their community. The influence of households' relative well-being in 1999 was the converse of the previous periods and may be explained in part by the fact that while real average consumption increased in 1993 and 1997, there was a slight decline in 1999 and households were more likely to classify themselves as poor.

For each additional child, the probability of the household classifying its consumption/income as more than adequate or belonging to the middle class decreases with a corresponding increase in the probability of the household classifying its consumption/income as less than adequate or being poor. This variable was, however, only significant in the earlier years of 1997 and 1993, while the *proportion of unemployed adults* was not significant during the period. The reason the number of children was no longer significant in 1999 is not clear, but this may be related to the growing number of elderly household members and the fact that the variable number of elderly became marginally significant in 1999.

The coefficient of the variable *union status* of the head was significant in 1999 and 1997. The results for 1997 indicate that *ceteris paribus*, heads who were married or living in a common law relationship had a higher probability of being in the middle class or enjoying consumption/income levels that were more than adequate. These heads had a lower probability of perceived poverty or consumption/income levels that were less than adequate, compared with heads who were single. This finding is consistent with the literature suggesting that married individuals are more likely to report higher well-being levels than their counterparts who are single. There is, however, a reversal in the results for 1999, and this is contrary to the established literature.

In this section, the number of subjectively poor households, based on self-assessment of their well-being status, were predicted. Households responded to different subjective questions based on both monetary and non-monetary indicators. They responded to the adequacy of income/food consumption and classified the household into different social classes. The responses are consistent with the money matrix approach to poverty measurement but undoubtedly captured some of the non-income dimensions of poverty. In the section that follows, the extent to which there is consistency in the households predicted as subjectively poor is assessed in comparison with households identified as poor, based on the objective income poverty line method.

Consistency: Objective and Subjective Poverty

Headcount indices have been reported for Jamaica by different studies using different methodologies. In some instances, these indices differ significantly, but no attempts have been made to establish the extent of overlap or to reconcile these differences. This section seeks to establish the extent to which headcount indices generated by different subjective methodologies are consistent with the headcount indices reported by the objective income poverty methods. Households who are classified as poor by both methods are referred to as unanimously poor.

If all households who identified themselves as poor are taken into consideration along with those who are classified as poor based on the objective method, 38.4 per cent, 25.5 per cent and 56.2 per cent of them were unanimously poor in 1999, 1997 and 1993, respectively (see table 4.3).[7] These results are not very sensitive to alternative assumptions of the level of economies of scales considered in this work. In the absence of economies of scales, the level of the headcount (objectively poor) increases, with a slight improvement in the proportion of households classified as poor by both methods. It is important to recognize that even if the estimates of the headcount reported by different methods are the same or comparable, as reported in Pradhan and Ravallion's (2000) study, there is no guarantee that the same households are being identified, and this underscores the differences in the methods. What is striking is the fact that virtually all households self-classified as not poor are objectively non-poor, but this fact is less so in the case of the community data.

As indicated above, in the community survey of 2002, data on the adequacy of food consumption and other basic needs were also collected.

Table 4.3 Consistency of the Subjective and Objective Poor

			Community 2002				Subjective									
	HHs Well-being groupings		Participatory Ranking		Adequate Food Consumption			1999 Class			1997 Adequate Income			1993 Adequate Food Consumption		
α = 0.15	Poor	Non-poor	Poor	Non-poor	Poor	Non-poor	Total	Poor	Non-poor	Total	Poor	Non-poor	Total	Poor	Non-poor	Total
Poor	76.3	22.2	73.6	72.9	95.8	69.7	73.4	38.4	0.4	16.9	25.5	0	17.0	56.2	0.1	15.8
Non-poor	23.7	77.8	26.4	27.1	4.2	30.3	26.6	61.6	99.6	83.1	74.5	100.0	83.0	43.8	99.9	84.2
N	161	8	121	48	23	146		824	1070		1348	672		538	1424	
Total	94.7	5.3	71.6	28.4	14.2	85.8		43.5	56.5		66.9	33.1		28.0	72.0	

(Objective)

Notes: (1) In Kingston Gardens members are generally known by aliases instead of their official names. This posed a problem since official names were given in the survey. At the PPA meeting, these official names were not easily recognized. The lone elderly person in the gathering knew all the households by their official names but not necessarily their alias. Subsequent attempts to match the outstanding official names with the aliases proved futile. (2) We control for difference in poverty incidence at a later stage in table 4.4.

Source: PIOJ 1993–2002.

So, too, were data on household self-assessment of their poverty status and community participatory well-being grouping. Questions on home production and gifts were not included in the questionnaire and were therefore estimated from the 1993–1999 JSLC data sets, scaled up by the average annual consumer price index. Consumption was adjusted by the regional average proportion of home production and gifts in per-adult equivalent consumption. In cases where households reported zero consumption, the relevant area mean of households in quintiles one was assigned. Following this adjustment, the estimated headcount for the communities decreased by approximately two percentage points.

The objective estimates were compared with the participatory community ranking and also point to differences in households identified as poor. Of those households classified as poor by the community, 73.6 per cent were also objectively poor. Similarly, table 4.3 shows that 76.3 per cent of households who classified themselves as poor were also objectively poor. For the sample as a whole, the proportion of households who were objectively poor and classified by the community and households as also poor respectively varied between 52.7 per cent and 72.2 per cent. This suggests that even though the headcount indices in the objective method and the community participatory method differed by just 1.8 percentage points, there are fundamental differences in the households each identifies as poor. Clearly, this has implications for policy, especially if the average characteristics of these households differed. Judged primarily on the basis of the headcount, the results of the community participatory methods accord much closer to the results of the objective method relative to the subjective ordering of households' well-being in the surveys. The community participatory and subjective ordering methods cannot be seen as substitutes, since results for the non-poor point to notable differences.

Households experiencing inadequate food consumption were all estimated to be poor based on the objective method (no account taken for economies of scales), and this is not surprising given the relative importance of food requirements in the objective poverty line. With adjustments made for economies of scale, it is found that the difference is not significant and the result is also robust for all scenarios of economies of scale.[8] What is of some concern, however, is the fact that these households only represent between 18.1 per cent and 20.5 per cent of households estimated as objectively poor, and therefore point to the lack of substitutability between the approaches. This also suggests, in keeping with the results of focus group meetings, that the attainment of food needs is not as great a problem in rural areas as is the acquisition of non-food essentials.

For the period prior to 2002, at most 0.4 per cent of households classified as subjectively non-poor were seen as objectively poor. This result is of interest since it is generally argued that the poor tend to overstate their consumption and, in some cases, may not classify themselves as poor. Although this practice is evident in the findings, the results are not conclusive. These results are clearly due to the different headcounts reported from the different methods and reflected in differences in scales between them. In order to control for the difference in the scales, the objective poverty line was adjusted to arrive at the exact headcount reported by the subjective method consistent with the relative methodologies.

Once the difference in scales is controlled for, a slightly different picture emerges (see table 4.4). The proportion of households self-classified as not poor but who, based on the objective method, are in fact poor, varied between 5.1 per cent in 1993 and 15.8 per cent in 1997. Estimates for the communities show greater levels of disparity, varying between 6.9 per cent and 68.8 per cent. The proportion of households self-classified as poor, but seen as not poor by the objective method, varied between 7.8 and 18.0 per cent for the period 1993–1999. Here again, there are greater levels of disparity for the communities and similar trends for alternative assumptions of economies of scale. What is hidden behind these percentages is the fact that once the scale effect is eliminated, the number of households classified as not poor but estimated as objectively poor was generally equal to the number of households self-classified as poor but seen as not poor by the objective method. This result held true for all the estimates generated and is seen in figure 4.1.

Table 4.4 also indicates that the proportion of households predicted as poor, based on household response to the questions on the adequacy of their food consumption, declined from 28.0 per cent in 1993 to 14.2 per cent in 2002. It is tempting to see the reduction in the proportion of households reporting inadequate food consumption between 1993 and 2002 as synonymous with a reduction in chronic poverty. This result does not support such a conclusion but, instead, points to the possible over-representation of rural communities in the 2002 survey. The results are

Table 4.4 Consistency of Subjective and Objective Poor Adjusted for Scale Effect

		Subjective																
		Community 2002									1999			1997			1993	
		HHs Well-being groupings			Participatory Community Ranking			Adequate Food Consumption			Class			Adequate Income			Adequate Food Consumption	
	$\alpha = 0.15$	Poor	Non-poor	Total	Poor	Non-poor	Total	Poor	Non-poor	Total	Poor	Non-poor	Total	Poor	Non-poor	Total	Poor	Non-poor	Total
Objective	Poor	96.9	55.6	94.7	72.7	68.8	71.6	58.3	6.9	14.2	82.0	14.4	43.5	92.2	15.8	66.9	86.9	5.1	28.0
	Non-poor	3.1	44.4	5.3	27.3	31.2	28.4	41.7	93.1	85.8	18.0	85.6	56.5	7.8	84.2	33.1	13.1	94.9	72.0
	N	160	9		121	48		24	145		819	1075		1351	669		550	1412	
	Total	94.7	5.3		71.6	28.4		14.2	85.8		43.5	56.5		66.9	33.1		28.0	72.0	

Source: PIOJ 1993–99.

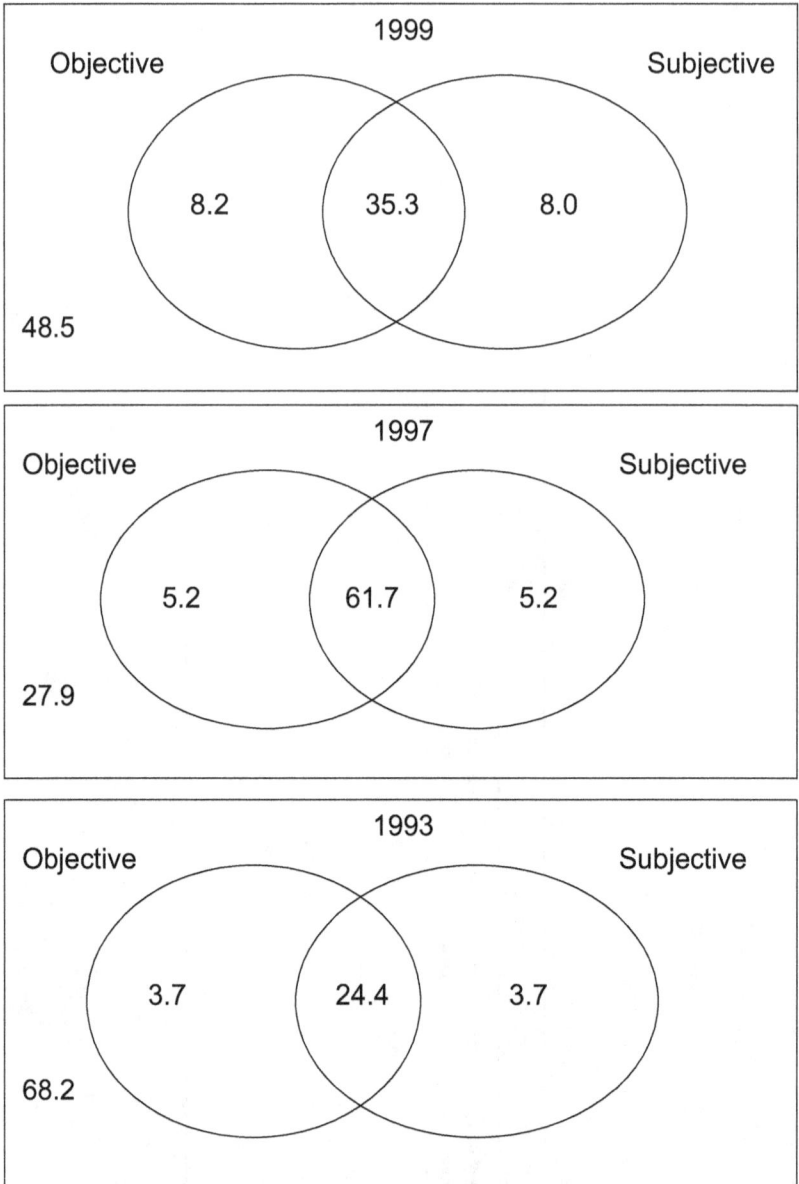

Figure 4.1   Distribution of households by poverty status

consistent since food needs are more likely to be met given the greater level of home production of food items, which are also acquired at a lower cost in rural areas. The difference in the proportion of households reporting less than adequate food consumption and being poor also suggests, as argued above, that the acquisition of other basic, non-food commodities may pose a greater challenge to these households in rural areas.

It is also not surprising that 94.7 per cent of households in the communities reported living in poverty. The reference point for these households was not just their consumption relative to that of other community members, but the state of their living conditions relative to non-community members. These households reside in communities that are relatively poor, where social amenities and physical infrastructure are either non-existent or in a state of disrepair and are generally below that found in urban centres. It was also established that households residing furthest from major commercial centres were more likely to classify themselves as poor. An interesting difference emerged in the community participatory ranking of households by community members. While the communities expressed views of their general living conditions relative to other communities and/or parishes, the actual ranking of households seemed to be more related to their relative well-being within the community. This fact seemed to have taken on a greater level of importance in the ranking of households by the community than in the actual assessment by households of their living conditions, hence the difference in the headcount reported for the household well-being ranking and community ranking of the same households. Discrepancies in the ranking of the same households by different groups are not uncommon, as illustrated by Chambers (1994b, 1259) referring to a village in India (the community versus a "professional" classification). According to Chambers (1994b), the two classifications coincided for 62 per cent of households, but further checks by Chambers revealed that for 92 per cent of the discrepancies, the community ranking of households was correct. Clearly, further research that goes beyond triangulation and seeks to understand such discrepancies is needed.[9]

These results highlight the extent to which households identified as subjectively poor overlap with the more objective approach – the extent to which households are unequivocally poor using both approaches – and point to a larger level of divergence in the approaches, and for the use of larger values of α.[10] These differences are largely due to the underlying differences in the methodologies used. While the objective method establishes a minimum standard based on nutritional attainment and other non-food essentials, it pays little or no attention to utility. At the same time, a household's decision to self-classify as poor is informed not just by current levels of consumption but by a number of other factors, including quality of social and community amenities, with no obvious account taken of nutritional standards. It is, therefore, possible that a household whose consumption is above the objective income poverty line may not spend enough on food as may be the case for those households who suggested that their food consumption was less than adequate. In such cases, the household may classify itself as poor, even if it could have spent enough on food by not spending on non-essential goods. In like manner, a household may deliberately suppress consumption in order to accumulate but, based on the objective threshold, is classified as poor, quite to the contrary of the household's own perception of its well-being. This suggests that the reasons some non-poor households may classify themselves as poor, while poor households classify themselves as not poor, can add information to improving the understanding of the concepts of poverty and vulnerability.

Conclusion

This chapter discussed predictions – based on established theory and household ranking of their own well-being – of the number of households that classified themselves as poor. These estimates were compared with the headcount index based on objective income poverty, and the degree of consistency or overlap established prior to and after adjustments had been made for difference in scales. Households that are poor on both fronts are classified as unanimously poor. These results will be unpacked further in chapter 5, which analyses the reasons households may classify themselves as poor. The next chapter presents an analysis of the correlates of consumption, contrasting the results for the pooled sample of all households with those for the poor and looking at how the results for the subjective poor compare with those for the objective poor.

Correlates of Household Well-Being

In keeping with the literature that supports models of poverty using data on household consumption, this chapter analyses the well-being of households. The variables that influence the well-being of households who have self-classified themselves as poor are contrasted with those for the objective poor and the pooled sample of all (poor and non-poor) households. The results of this work suggest that the factors that are correlated with the well-being of subjectively poor households are consistent with those for the pooled sample of all households, but there are noticeable differences for the variables *child dependency ratio* and *single-female-headed households*. As previously indicated, these results also suggest that differences between the reasons households classify themselves as subjectively poor and the correlates of objective poverty may not be correlated with consumption. In other words, there are some factors that influence households to classify themselves as subjectively poor that are not influenced by their level of consumption. The results in this chapter also provide the context within which to understand the results in chapters 6 and 7.

The chapter begins by identifying the theoretical issues in modelling the correlates of household well-being. The debate surrounding the advantages and disadvantages of modelling consumption is discussed. The methodological issues identified in this section are also relevant to chapters 6 and 7. The factors that are associated with household consumption are then analysed, dividing the sample into subjectively and objectively poor households. In the last section, the conclusion points to the main findings and implications.

Modelling the Well-Being of Households

In keeping with the debate about poverty functions, a multiple regression was specified in which the log of per-adult equivalent consumption for objectively poor households, subjectively poor households and the pooled sample of all households are regressed on a number of socio-economic variables. In chapters 6 and 7, probit models are specified to understand the determinants of poverty and subjective well-being. The two types of models are conceptually different but can be used complementarily to understand the well-being of households, establish the difference between objective and subjective approaches to poverty measurement, and provide reasons some non-poor households may define themselves as poor.

By estimating a function involving only the poor, the data are truncated, thus losing information about the non-poor (Appleton 1995). However, this is corrected by pooling the poor and non-poor, making it possible to establish the extent to which the correlates of consumption for the poor are different from the general population. This approach, however, assumes that the poor and non-poor are not fundamentally different since the model imposes constant parameters over the entire distribution, assuming that the influence of different household characteristics is the same for the poor and non-poor.[1] This cannot be justified if the poor tend to face different risks, constraints and returns to their endowments. This line of argument supports the use of dichotomous dependent variable models, used in chapters 6 and 7, or estimating sub-samples, as will be done in this chapter. The use of probit models is further supported due to possible measurement errors that can arise from the calculation of consumption or income from household surveys (Appleton 1995).

The motivation for estimating both consumption (continuous) and poverty (dichotomous) functions is that the consumption regression is preferable – though some may argue otherwise – to the dichotomous. When analysing objective poverty, however, the subjective poverty regression is necessarily dichotomous. Since it is better to estimate continuous models for the objective measure, it is first necessary in this chapter to estimate these models for both objective and subjective poverty and to establish in the following two chapters that the continuous and dichotomous models for both measures of poverty do not give widely different results.[2]

Here the consumption functions for both the objective and subjective poor are compared using ordinary least squares models as specified:

$$y_i = \beta_0 + \beta_i x_i + \varepsilon_i \qquad (5.1)$$

It is necessary to establish the relationship between log per-adult equivalent consumption expenditure and a number of independent variables, where ε, the error term, is assumed to be identical and independently distributed, y_i is the log of adult equivalent per capita consumption adjusted for economies of scale ($\alpha = 0.15$ being the reference level) and x_i, households' characteristics. For each year there are three separate models, two of which use observations only for the poor established by the subjective and objective methods, and the other uses the full sample of all households.

Correlates of Consumption and Poverty

This section analyses the factors that are correlated with consumption generally, as well as for the objective and subjective poor households. The models include many obviously endogenous variables which are correlates of poverty, not determinants, such as *radio*, *stereo* and *television* (the covariance matrices of all the right-hand side variables showed weak correlations). These variables are included for two reasons: (1) they influence households' perception of their own well-being and, since the purpose is to compare subjective versus objective well-being, then all variables included in the former models are necessarily included in the latter, and (2) these variables are of interest for use in models with good predictive fit for targeting purposes.

The variables used in the consumption functions are classified under four general groups of capital – human, social, financial and physical – since these are seen as important means through which households may emerge from poverty. The results from the models are reported in tables 5.1.a, 5.1.b

Table 5.1a   Ordinary Least Squares Results for Natural Log of Consumption Expenditure, 1999

	(1)	(2)	(3)		(1)	(2)	(3)
GENDER	0.077	0.132	0.029	AGRIWORK	−0.035	0.023	0.130
	0.035*	0.051**	0.062		0.033	0.037	0.050*
CHIDEPEND	0.008	0.044	−0.005	PERUEMP	−0.191	−0.107	−0.085
	0.017	0.019*	0.023		0.061**	0.053*	0.077
OLDDEPEND	−0.123	−0.116	0.065	SEWMACH	0.032	0.007	0.074
	0.039**	0.047*	0.054		0.030	0.048	0.074
HHSIZE	−0.131	−0.104	−0.017	GSTOVE	0.127	0.118	0.101
	0.013**	0.017**	0.038		0.035**	0.039**	0.058+
HHSIZESQ	0.004	0.005	0.001	ESTOVE	0.115	−0.043	−0.061
	0.001**	0.001**	0.003		0.102	0.248	0.137
HHAGE	−0.004	−0.001	0.000	FRIDGE	0.065	0.098	0.096
	0.003	0.004	0.006		0.031*	0.035**	0.066
HHAGESQ	−0.000	−0.000	−0.000	RADIO	−0.003	0.026	0.039
	0.000	0.000	0.000		0.026	0.034	0.046
DISABLE	−0.078	−0.048	−0.134	STEREO	0.062	0.138	0.103
	0.083	0.093	0.118		0.032+	0.054*	0.095
SINGLEHH	0.025	0.213	0.036	VIDEO	0.039	0.027	0.095
	0.039	0.052**	0.067		0.030	0.042	0.087
PARTNER	0.139	−0.004	−0.036	WASHMACH	0.105	0.028	−0.260
	0.062*	0.115	0.131		0.046*	0.140	0.102*
URBAN	0.080	−0.020	−0.045	TV	0.020	0.014	−0.077
	0.055	0.064	0.093		0.037	0.042	0.074
REMITTANCE	0.072	0.123	0.117	VEHICLES	0.300	−0.132	−0.139
	0.032*	0.038**	0.053*		0.039**	0.102	0.090
FOSTERIN	0.045	−0.004	−0.022	URBREMIT	−0.073	−0.028	−0.018
	0.039	0.044	0.065		0.046	0.060	0.081
SUPPORT	−0.095	−0.085	0.103	URBFOSTER	−0.091	0.085	0.015
	0.038*	0.042*	0.063		0.050+	0.059	0.085
ROOMS	0.002	−0.040	0.035	URBSUPPT	0.015	0.025	−0.024
	0.024	0.028	0.041		0.056	0.062	0.085
ROOMSQ	0.001	0.003	−0.006	URBWATER	0.016	0.187	0.311
	0.003	0.003	0.004		0.060	0.068**	0.097**
WATER	−0.106	−0.130	−0.179	URBTENURE	−0.061	−0.011	0.005
	0.034**	0.038**	0.065**		0.048	0.058	0.079
TENURE	0.040	0.124	0.099	URBTELE	0.156	−0.008	−0.026
	0.035	0.041**	0.053+		0.057**	0.067	0.088
TELEPH	0.133	0.040	0.071	URBLIGHT	−0.081	−0.129	−0.064
	0.040**	0.046	0.073		0.069	0.069+	0.078
LIGHTING	−0.154	−0.068	0.016	URBSHTCH	0.058	0.062	0.040
	0.050**	0.050	0.054		0.065	0.070	0.113
SHRKITCH	−0.060	−0.027	−0.058	Constant	11.797	11.039	10.482
	0.049	0.050	0.065		0.092**	0.115**	0.252**
BASEDUC	−0.265	−0.033	−0.173				
	0.044**	0.056	0.178	Number of Obs.	1838	795	304
SECEDUC	−0.180	0.035	−0.074	R-squared	0.53	0.37	0.27
	0.044**	0.054	0.182	F Statistic	47.3	12.1	2.35
SERVWORK	0.032	0.048	0.072	Prob> F	0.000	0.000	0.000
	0.027	0.035	0.059				

Notes: (1) Models 1, 2 and 3 refer to the pooled sample, households self-classified as poor (subjective) and objective poor respectively; (2) robust standard errors are reported in italics and are used as a means of solving the problem of heteroscedasticity suggested by the Breusch-Pagan/Cook-Weisberg tests; (3) +, * and ** indicate significance at 10 per cent, 5 per cent and 1 per cent respectively; (4) the variable health insurance was dropped due to possible multicollinearity.

Table 5.1b Ordinary Least Squares Results for Natural Log of Consumption Expenditure, 1997

	(1)	(2)	(3)		(1)	(2)	(3)
GENDER	0.066	0.058	0.045	SERVWORK	0.004	0.030	0.087
	*0.032**	*0.032+*	*0.051*		*0.024*	*0.026*	*0.050+*
CHIDEPEND	0.013	−0.009	0.002	AGRIWORK	−0.013	0.034	0.074
	0.016	*0.016*	*0.026*		*0.034*	*0.033*	*0.052*
OLDDEPEND	0.003	0.015	−0.068	PERUEMP	−0.123	−0.132	0.062
	0.039	*0.042*	*0.068*		*0.052**	*0.049***	*0.066*
HHSIZE	−0.166	−0.043	0.021	SEWMACH	−0.051	0.009	0.018
	*0.016***	*0.015***	*0.023*		*0.031*	*0.034*	*0.061*
HHSIZESQ	0.008	0.001	−0.001	GSTOVE	0.149	0.175	0.114
	*0.001***	*0.001*	*0.002*		*0.032***	*0.030***	*0.048**
HHAGE	−0.001	−0.003	−0.001	ESTOVE	0.130	−0.160	−0.037
	0.003	*0.003*	*0.006*		*0.117*	*0.154*	*0.096*
HHAGESQ	−0.000	−0.000	0.000	FRIDGE	0.033	0.043	−0.001
	*0.000**	*0.000*	*0.000*		*0.031*	*0.031*	*0.063*
DISABLE	−0.252	−0.176	−0.105	RADIO	0.050	0.071	0.098
	*0.070***	*0.064***	*0.078*		*0.027+*	*0.028***	*0.041**
SINGLEHH	0.032	0.085	0.027	STEREO	0.065	0.056	−0.053
	0.036	*0.038**	*0.063*		*0.032**	*0.039*	*0.125*
PARTNER	0.100	0.016	−0.141	VIDEO	0.101	0.071	0.019
	0.054+	*0.054*	*0.181*		*0.029***	*0.033**	*0.089*
URBAN	0.185	0.042	0.045	WASHMACH	0.042	−0.046	0.000
	*0.052***	*0.054*	*0.086*		*0.052*	*0.081*	*0.000*
HHINSUR	0.204	0.137	−0.003	TV	0.032	0.052	0.025
	*0.054***	*0.054**	*0.069*		*0.032*	*0.031+*	*0.052*
REMITTANCE	0.081	0.064	0.027	VEHICLES	0.343	0.190	0.217
	*0.033**	*0.033**	*0.057*		*0.041***	*0.048***	*0.115+*
FOSTERIN	0.042	0.062	−0.015	URBHINSU	−0.094	−0.129	−0.140
	0.037	*0.037+*	*0.055*		*0.064*	*0.074+*	*0.193*
SUPPORT	−0.038	0.002	0.024	URBREMIT	−0.014	0.039	0.164
	0.037	*0.036*	*0.051*		*0.046*	*0.049*	*0.082**
ROOMS	0.048	−0.029	−0.109	URBFOSTER	0.027	0.034	−0.076
	*0.020**	*0.026*	*0.058+*		*0.052*	*0.050*	*0.090*
ROOMSQ	−0.002	0.004	0.011	URBSUPP	−0.039	−0.017	−0.171
	0.002	*0.003*	*0.007*		*0.052*	*0.053*	*0.084**
WATER	−0.107	−0.117	−0.020	URBWATER	0.055	0.137	0.181
	*0.034***	*0.034***	*0.048*		*0.057*	*0.055**	*0.092**
TENURE	0.043	0.009	0.030	URBTENURE	−0.096	−0.015	−0.010
	0.035	*0.035*	*0.049*		*0.047**	*0.046*	*0.081*
TELEPH	0.031	0.004	−0.009	URBTELE	0.185	0.172	0.174
	0.043	*0.043*	*0.058*		*0.054***	*0.056***	*0.094+*
LIGHTING	−0.068	−0.025	−0.048	URBLIGHT	−0.182	−0.126	−0.028
	0.043	*0.040*	*0.052*		*0.066***	*0.060**	*0.095*
SHRKITCH	−0.005	0.069	−0.092	URBSHTCH	−0.026	−0.027	0.091
	0.068	*0.072*	*0.125*		*0.077*	*0.083*	*0.141*
BELBASED	−0.380	−0.214	−0.402	Constant	11.535	10.961	10.457
	*0.131***	*0.116+*	*0.184**		*0.098***	*0.112***	*0.180***
BASICED	−0.341	−0.085	−0.262				
	*0.056***	*0.081*	*0.099***	Number of Obs.	1891	1275	327
SECEDUC	−0.263	−0.055	−0.314	R-squared	0.56	0.37	0.23
	*0.052***	*0.081*	*0.116***	F statistic	56.2	19.4	1.75
				Prob> F	0.000	0.000	0.003

Notes: (1) Models 1, 2 and 3 refer to the pooled sample, subjective and objective poor respectively; (2) robust standard errors are reported in italics and are used as a means of solving the problem of heteroscedasticity suggested by the Breusch-Pagan/Cook-Weisberg tests; (3) +, * and ** indicate significance at 10 per cent, 5 per cent and 1 per cent respectively.

Table 5.1c Ordinary Least Squares Results for Natural Log of Consumption Expenditure, 1993

	(1)	(2)	(3)		(1)	(2)	(3)
GENDER	0.040	0.054	0.046	AGRIWORK	−0.053	0.016	0.095
	0.027	0.041	0.051		0.033	0.047	0.052+
CHIDEPEND	−0.056	0.042	−0.030	PERUEMP	−0.172	−0.079	−0.091
	0.017**	0.024+	0.031		0.056**	0.075	0.089
OLDDEPEND	0.062	0.069	0.119	SEWMACH	−0.032	0.030	−0.017
	0.034+	0.049	0.053*		0.030	0.060	0.081
HHSIZE	−0.149	0.017	0.009	GSTOVE	0.182	0.031	0.017
	0.014**	0.022	0.036		0.031**	0.043	0.048
HHSIZESQ	0.009	0.000	−0.002	ESTOVE	0.275	—	—
	0.001**	0.002	0.003		0.119*		
HHAGE	−0.001	−0.000	−0.007	FRIDGE	0.091	0.060	0.076
	0.004	0.007	0.009		0.031**	0.045	0.060
HHAGESQ	−0.000	−0.000	0.000	RADIO	0.058	0.059	−0.015
	0.000+	0.000	0.000		0.028*	0.041	0.049
DISABLE	−0.244	−0.030	0.088	STEREO	0.093	−0.075	−0.270
	0.074**	0.069	0.078		0.039*	0.118	0.159+
SINGLEHH	0.050	0.131	0.048	VIDEO	0.064	0.025	0.021
	0.035	0.055*	0.074		0.030*	0.073	0.091
PARTNER	0.089	−0.061	−0.029	WASHMACH	0.326	—	—
	0.028**	0.051	0.057		0.078**		
URBAN	0.014	0.081	0.371	TV	0.071	0.103	0.136
	0.086	0.133	0.138**		0.033*	0.047*	0.058*
HHINSUR	0.227	0.301	0.380	VEHICLES	0.274	0.200	0.000
	0.065**	0.089**	0.094**		0.039**	0.113+	0.000
REMITTANCE	0.023	0.053	0.094	URBHINSU	−0.088	−0.116	−0.078
	0.033	0.043	0.050+		0.072	0.144	0.162
FOSTERIN	−0.027	−0.023	0.059	URBREMIT	0.038	0.046	−0.062
	0.040	0.047	0.050		0.046	0.069	0.086
SUPPORT	0.019	0.088	0.098	URBFOSTER	0.125	0.105	−0.046
	0.037	0.049+	0.057+		0.058*	0.086	0.118
ROOMS	0.080	0.003	0.036	URBSUPP	−0.134	−0.149	−0.142
	0.029**	0.043	0.047		0.060*	0.088+	0.103
ROOMSQ	−0.007	−0.005	−0.004	URBWATER	0.004	0.067	0.026
	0.004+	0.005	0.005		0.059	0.077	0.100
WATER	−0.105	−0.126	−0.150	URBNTENURE	−0.043	−0.122	−0.313
	0.034**	0.049*	0.059*		0.082	0.120	0.126*
TENURE	0.014	0.149	0.276	URBTELE	−0.050	0.167	0.000
	0.070	0.107	0.109*		0.063	0.151	0.000
TELEPH	0.229	−0.031	0.175	URBLIGHT	−0.036	−0.111	−0.058
	0.055**	0.112	0.139		0.058	0.073	0.097
LIGHTING	−0.052	0.009	0.079	URBSHTCH	−0.058	0.015	0.015
	0.042	0.055	0.066		0.073	0.110	0.163
SHRKITCH	0.023	0.041	−0.020	Constant	10.615	9.551	9.442
	0.059	0.084	0.129		0.137**	0.213**	0.268**
BELBASED	−0.352	−0.542	−0.590				
	0.123**	0.186**	0.189**	Number of Obs.	1904	532	305
BASICED	−0.090	−0.245	−0.199	R-squared	0.52	0.26	0.24
	0.040*	0.061**	0.078*	F Statistic	45.9	8.4	1.89
SECEDUC	−0.109	−0.293	−0.245	Prob > F	0.000	0.000	0.002
	0.040**	0.068**	0.103*				
SERVWORK	0.044	0.095	0.073				
	0.025+	0.045*	0.060				

Notes: (1) Models 1, 2 and 3 refer to the pooled sample, subjective and objective poor respectively;
(2) robust standard errors are reported in italics and are used as a means of solving the problem of heteroscedasticity suggested by the Breusch-Pagan/Cook-Weisberg tests;
(3) +, * and ** indicate significance at 10 per cent, 5 per cent and 1 per cent respectively.

and 5.1.c. The best fit is obtained by using the semi-log model, where the dependent variable is the natural logarithm of per-adult equivalent consumption expenditure, adjusted for economies of scales at the lower limit suggested in the literature. In the following sections, the results are analysed within the framework of the four groups of capital.

Human Capital

The literature on human capital tends to focus on adequate nutrition and the influence of variables such as education and health on household well-being (Booth et al. 1998, 73–75). The literature also points to the interaction between human capital and other forms of capital (World Bank 2000), suggesting that it is not possible at all times to clearly distinguish human capital from other forms of capital. In addition to these variables, other household demographic variables important in determining labour force participation and household disposable income are included. Some of the variables used in this analysis – such as *union status of household head* – may not be easily categorized under any one form of capital.

Gender and Union Status of Household Head

The *gender of the household head* and *union status* do not significantly influence the level of consumption of objectively poor households. This result does not hold for the pooled sample and for households self-classified as poor. The data for 1999 and 1997 indicate that male-headed households, on average, consumed 7.5 per cent more than female-headed households. The average difference in consumption levels between these households is somewhat greater, at 10 per cent for households self-classified as poor. Households headed by females who are single, in a visiting relationship or have no relationship (single-female-headed households) consume on average 15.4 per cent more than all other households.[3] The consumption levels of the objective poor are not statistically different for any of the years under consideration. This is seen in table 5.2, through the comparison between the average consumption of male-headed households, that of female-headed households and that of single-female-headed households. The finding seems contrary to

Table 5.2   Per-Adult Equivalent Consumption, 1993–1999

	Mean		
	Pooled	Subjective	Objective
	1999		
SFHHs	89,064.9	51,937.9	27,576.2
FHHs	85,949.8	49,178.6	27,628.2
MHHs	10,3455.6	47,501.7	29,657.1
	1997		
SFHHs	78,272.4	50,095.6	23,515.4
FHHs	73,905.6	48,152.2	23,345.8
MHHs	85,205.0	46,374.8	23,613.7
	1993		
SFHHs	35,644.0	13,444.2	10,228.0
FHHs	30,585.9	12,570.9	9,536.4
MHHs	33,908.3	12,434.5	9,630.3

Source: PIOJ 1993–99.

the general established literature on the well-being of female-headed households, but it supports the thesis that married individuals are more likely to report higher levels of well-being relative to those who are single. This finding is discussed further in chapters 6 and 7.

Dependants

This section analyses the results of the child dependency ratio. The direction of influence on consumption of the *child dependency ratio*, which is the proportion of children per working age adults within the household, is not consistent across models and the period under study. For the general population, a one-unit increase in the *child dependency ratio*, ceteris paribus, significantly reduces household consumption by 5.6 per cent. This result is only supported by the data for 1993 and is consistent with the direction of influence of the variable for the objective poor. For households

Table 5.3   Reasons for Children's Absence from School, 1999

Reason for absence from school	Any given day n = 499	Fridays n = 180
Illness	4.23	–
Truancy	0.65	2.15
Working outside the home	1.1	1.1
Needed at home	1.85	5.38
Market day	0.43	1.08
Transportation problems	2.71	–
School closed	4.45	–
Shoes/uniform missing/dirty/wet	0.54	–
Rain	0.54	–
Money problems	12.81	79.57
Had to run an errand	0.87	–
Other	69.82	10.75

Source: PIOJ 1999.

self-classified as poor, a one-unit increase in the *child dependency ratio* significantly increased consumption in 1999 and 1993 by 4.4 per cent and 4.2 per cent respectively. The result for 1993 is, however, marginally significant. Does this suggest the likelihood that children's goods are more expensive than adult goods or the impact of programmes geared towards helping poor households with children? It is not possible to establish the share of household budget spent on children's goods, and the benefit received from the Food Stamp Programme is generally very low. More importantly, this result points to the phenomenon of increased levels of child participation in economic activities to supplement the income of their families, and supports Ennew and Young's argument that Jamaican "children are mostly engaged in casual work which may best be described as strategies for obtaining cash rather than employment" (1981, 24). This is evident in the growing number of children involved in petty trading and menial tasks on the streets of major commercial centres.

In support of this fact, and borne out by the data, are the high levels of non-attendance of primary and secondary school children, especially boys, on Fridays (56 per cent of children absent on Fridays are boys), with the main reason cited as money problems.[4] Table 5.3 shows that on any given day, 12.8 per cent of school children's absence is due to *money problems*. The category *Other* is the most important reason for absence on any given day and possibly reflects the reluctance of parents to admit that child labour was the reason. The possible reluctance of households to admit to the existence of child labour is also seen in the small percentage of households identifying the reason for absence as being due to *working outside the home*, *market day* and *needed at home*. It is also likely that, given the large proportion of children absent due to *money problems* on Fridays, one can expect that they will be involved in some form of economic activity if they are to return to school the following week.

While the above discussion assesses the reasons for absence on any given day and on Fridays, it is important to assess the number of days children are absent over some time frame, to give an indication of their involvement in child labour. This is done by using the reported efforts of parents to send children to school during a reference period of twenty school days as a proxy for attendance. Children are sent to school, on average, for sixteen days, and just over one-third are sent every day. There is no difference in the average number of days of attendance (fifteen days) of children per household, and this is not significantly sensitive to the gender of the household head or union status.[5] Clearly, the preparation for market day, home duties and the opportunities for selling goods at the start of the weekend also lure children away from school. These households, even if they are above the objective poverty line, given their dependence on their children to supplement income/consumption and their inability to keep them in school, are not surprisingly classifying themselves as poor. This result is also seen in the case of Rajasthan, India, where village informants deem themselves poor when they cannot afford to send their children to school (Krishna 2004), and it is also consistent with the results from the Jamaican community well-being rankings.

This situation clearly begs the question of how substantial have the earnings from child labour been to have contributed so significantly to household consumption. One may also question the role played by various forms of support mechanisms, such as remittances, child support, and support from friends and relatives, in influencing this result and the extent to which the receipt of these are motivated by the presence and number of children in the household. Clearly, there is no conclusive answer to these concerns, and further research is needed to isolate the various support mechanisms and coping/survival strategies employed by households and their contribution to household well-being. The contribution of child support to household consumption expenditure may provide some insights. For households self-classified as poor, child support represented 3.2 per cent, 25.5 per cent and 22.6 per cent of total consumption for 1993, 1997 and 1999, respectively, compared with an average of 5.1 per cent for the non-poor, and may be one of the factors influencing this result and the decision of these households to classify themselves as poor.

Following the same logic for the inclusion of the *child dependency ratio*, the *elderly dependency ratio* was included as an independent variable. The 1999 data conforms to the general expectation that an increase in the *elderly dependency ratio* is associated with a reduction in consumption. This result is true for the general sample and for households self-classified as poor. There is a reversal of the influence of the variable on consumption of households estimated to be objectively poor in 1993. The reason for this result is not clear. However, it could indicate the fact that some elderly individuals may continue in the labour market beyond age sixty-five, and this fact, coupled with possible returns from previous investments, may mean that they will continue to contribute positively to household well-being.

Having looked at the composition of the household, the influence of household size is now examined.

Household Size

The 1999, 1997 and 1993 data for the pooled sample conclusively support the thesis that household size has a significant influence on consumption. The square of household size is included to control for non-linear effects, and it is also highly significant. An additional household member reduces consumption by an average of 13.2 per cent. At the lower limit of economies used in this study, neither of these variables significantly influences consumption for those households estimated to be objectively poor. For households self-classified as poor, however, both variables are significant in 1999 alone, but while the sign of the square of household size is consistent with expectations, it is not significant in 1997. For households self-classified as poor, an additional member reduced consumption by 9.4 per cent in 1999 and approximately 4.2 per cent in 1997. Given the positive sign on the square of the corresponding variable, the reducing effect is true only up to a certain point, after which greater numbers actually have a reverse effect, with the function exhibiting a concave relationship. The average minima for the pooled sample is twelve members, while for the subjective poor in 1999, it is eleven members. The fact that household size is not a significant correlate of consumption for the objectively poor is clearly due to the small allowance for economies of scale and is consistent with the literature on the importance of household size in any poverty profile, once allowance is made for economies of scale (White and Masset 2003). In fact, household size appears more important when there is no allowance for economies of scale.

Disability and Age of Household Head

Households whose heads have some form of *disability* generally tend to consume at lower levels than those households whose heads have no disability. This result was significant for both the pooled sample and subjectively poor households in 1997, but significant only for the pooled sample in 1993. In the general population, these households consumed an average of 22 per cent less than other households, while the subjectively poor households consumed 16.1 per cent less. On the other hand, the consumption level among the objectively poor was not significantly different from the average of all households.[6]

Age and age square of the head are included in the analysis to capture experience and the stage in the life cycle of the household (Grootaert, Kanbur and Oh 1997). The data suggest that, generally, neither the *age of the household head* nor the square of this variable is a significant correlate of consumption, suggesting the absence of a life-cycle effect in poverty or perceived well-being (Mukherjee and Benson 2003). The signs on both variables are generally negative and counter-intuitive. Consumption is expected to increase with the age of the household head, albeit at a declining rate, before declining at the higher end of the age distribution in keeping with the permanent income hypothesis and results of earnings functions for Jamaica generated by Hotchkiss and Moore (1996). As a result, these variables were dropped (using the 1999 data) but there was no effect (as regards the signs of the coefficients or level of significance) on the other variables in the pooled sample or for the objectively poor, while the effects for the subjectively poor were far from dramatic. In this case, only two variables that were previously not significant became marginally significant, retaining the same signs of their coefficients – basic education (represented as *BASEDUC*) and *ROOMS*. The variable proportion of household members unemployed (represented as *PERUEMP*), which was previously significant, became marginally significant but retained the same sign. The relationship between *age* and the square of this term with these variables is not clear.

Thus far, the composition and size of the household and characteristics of the household head have been covered. This was done based on the expectation that the head embodies some level of productive asset, which, in turn, influences the characteristics of the household. Now, the quality of this asset is controlled for through looking at their educational attainment.

Education of Principal Earner

Three dummy variables relating to *basic*, *secondary* and *tertiary* levels of education are included in the models, the reference category being *principal earner with tertiary education*. The principal earner is used instead of the household head since headship in the context of Jamaica is not necessarily associated with the main decision-maker. The eldest adult in the household may be assigned headship regardless of authority or economic contribution, so headship may not accurately reflect the person with the most decision-making authority within the household. Based on the 1999 data, 70.2 per cent of the heads are also the principal earners; the corresponding proportions for female and male heads are 58.0 per cent and 79.0 per cent respectively. In 10.4 per cent of households, the spouse of the nominated head is the principal earner.

In 1999, the number of principal earners with no formal academic education was relatively small and was merged with the category *basic education*. The explanatory power of the educational dummies for the principal earner is relatively large and generally significant. Principal earners with either no formal education, basic and/or secondary-level education, generally consume significantly less than those who have had a tertiary education. This result, however, does not hold for households self-classified as poor in 1999 and 1997 or for objectively poor households in 1999. This is possibly due to the small number of individuals with tertiary education in these categories and less variation in the education attainment of the principal earner of these households.

In terms of a summary of the influence of human capital on household consumption, the gender and union status of the household head, child and elderly dependants, household size and a number of characteristics of the head/principal earner of the household influence the level of consumption of households self-classified as poor and the pooled sample of all households, but there are noticeable differences. The direction of influence of the child dependency ratio is different and suggests that households may classify themselves as poor because of the involvement of their children in child labour. In addition, of households self-classified as poor, single-female-headed households consume significantly more than the excluded categories, while for the pooled sample, male-headed households consume significantly more than female-headed households. To the extent that single-female-headed households' level of consumption is attained by the involvement of children in child labour, it is not surprising that they are classifying themselves as poor. Few of the above variables significantly influenced the consumption of objectively poor households, and in such cases, their influence was generally consistent with the expectation.

Social Capital

Social capital concerns the relationships and networks that link individuals and facilitate cooperation for mutual benefit. They may also be manifested in the level and type of support received by households from both community members and relatives who reside elsewhere (Moser and Holland 1997; World Bank 2000; Booth et al. 1998). According to Honig (1996) the extent and effectiveness of social and community relations can modify the returns to human capital: social networks provided by extended family or community-based relationships are likely to augment the effects of education, facilitate the most advantageous accumulation of resources and utilization of skills.

This section focuses on the support received from relatives and friends residing elsewhere. The analysis begins with the impact of the *place of*

residence of the spouse, support from friends and relatives living in Jamaica,
support from family and friends living abroad and finally the receipt of
child support for children living within the household – those children
who are *fostered-in.*

The place of residence of a spouse or partner did not significantly affect
the level of consumption of both households estimated as poor and those
self-classified as poor. For the pooled sample, however, households whose
head's partner resided outside of the home experienced a positive effect
on their consumption, which is also significant for all years, although only
marginally in 1997. The positive influence of this variable may reflect the
migration of household members to urban centres or other countries and,
therefore, the extent to which this variable is correlated with *remittances*
from friends and family residing in a foreign country, fostered-in, and *support*
from friends and family residing in Jamaica requires consideration. However, the data reveal very weak correlations.

For the pooled sample and for households self-classified as poor, the data
for 1999 show that households in receipt of *support from friends and fam-*
ily residing in Jamaica tend to consume significantly less, approximately 9
per cent less, than those not in receipt of this form of support. Clearly, there
is a possible endogeneity problem, with poor households receiving support
because they are poor. This is not a problem given the research intentions,
and, in fact, *support from friends and family* in 1993 was positively associated with the level of consumption of households subjectively and objectively
poor. These coefficients are, however, only marginally significant. The data
also point to relatively lower levels of consumption of households in urban
centres in receipt of this type of assistance, and this is significant for the
pooled sample and the subjective poor in 1993 but only for the objective poor
in 1997. The reason for this benevolence to relatively less well-off households
is not clear, but it clearly points to the importance of social capital.

The receipt of remittances has a positive and significant influence
on consumption for all groups of households, with a greater percentage
increase for the poor. Generally, there is no regional difference in the influence of remittances on consumption, and only in the case of the objective
poor in 1997 did urban dwellers who received this form of support consume significantly more than their counterparts in rural areas.

Households received support for children whose parent(s) live elsewhere,
and, in approximately one-third of the cases where households received this

form of assistance, it was for the child of the head. In some cases, the head was a grandparent. Nonetheless, this refers to the total children for whom monies are received as *fostered-in*. The *fostering-in* of individuals within the household does not, at a conventional level, significantly affect the level of household consumption, and the relative direction of influence on urban households is not consistent. While the 1999 data points to relatively lower levels of consumption by urban households who foster-in children, the data for 1993 suggest a significant reversal of influence.

Consistent with expectations, this section shows that social capital has a positive influence on the well-being of households. This is seen in the positive influence of the place of residence of a spouse for the pooled sample of households. In addition, the receipt of support from friends and family living in Jamaica had a positive influence on the well-being of poor households (though not in all cases), pointing to a tendency of better-off households helping less fortunate ones. This is also seen in the influence of remittances on household well-being.

Financial Capital

This form of capital tends to focus on household savings and access to credit, but the variables included under this section may be seen as some of the preconditions affecting the attainment of financial capital – the *education of the head*, the *sector of employment of the principal earner* and the *proportion of adults unemployed*.

Industry/Occupation of Principal Earner and Employment Status

The industries where the principal earners mainly work[7] included in the analysis are *services* (clerks, protective service workers, street vendors and helpers, labourers, and sales persons) and *agriculture* (farmers, loggers, fishermen and hunters). These are compared with *mining, manufacture, electricity, gas and water, construction and installation, wholesale and retail trade, hotels and restaurants, transport, storage and communication, financing, insurance, real estate* and *business services (the comparison group)*. For both 1999 and 1997, the data show that the sector of employment of the principal earner was not a significant variable affecting the consumption of the pooled sample or households self-classified as poor. While this remained the case for *agricultural* workers in 1993, when compared with the comparison group, *service* workers consumed 4.4 per cent and 9.5 per cent more respectively. It is not clear why service workers had a higher level of consumption and what part the deepening of macro-economic liberalization efforts and fiscal prudence of 1991 may have contributed to this result.

For objectively poor households whose principal earners were employed in the agricultural sector, their consumption was significantly greater than the comparison group in 1999 and 1993, consuming 5.0 per cent and 5.2 per cent more respectively. In addition, those households whose principal earners were employed in the service sector in 1997 also consumed significantly more than the comparison group. With the exception of the result for 1999, the results for the other periods are marginally significant. These households possibly consume more, since the other categories of the poor are perhaps employed in fixed-income, low-paying jobs and, relative to the agriculture and service workers (informal sector workers included), they may not have the same level of flexibility to engage in multiple income-earning strategies. In fact, community focus group meetings point to the multiple income-earning activities in which households may be involved. For instance, small-scale farmers shift not only between hill and low-land farming but also between working on neighbouring estates and self-employed activities. Anderson and Witter (1994, 4) suggest a historical relationship between the plantations and small-scale farmers whereby wage earners moved between these areas of occupation, and this movement was affected by the expansion and contraction of the plantations.

Next, the influence of employment status on household consumption expenditure is analysed. According to Smith (1962), the average household in Jamaica is likely to be composed of more than two adult members and, as such, the proportion of employed adults may be more relevant than the employment status of the household head/spouse. The effect of the proportion of unemployed adults on household well-being is therefore analysed. The proportion of household members in the labour market who were unemployed had a significant and negative influence on the general level of consumption of the pooled sample. A one-unit increase in the proportion of unemployed individuals results in an average reduction in consumption of 15 per cent. This result resonates with that for households self-classified as poor, resulting in a decline in consumption of 11.3 per cent.

This variable, however, does not significantly affect the level of consumption of the objective poor and points to the fact that many of the poor classified as unemployed are instead underemployed.

This section has shown that the sector of employment of the principal earner and the proportion of unemployed adults influence household well-being. The results for the pooled sample and households self-classified as poor are generally consistent. However, while the sector of employment of the principal earner had a positive influence on the well-being of poor households, compared with the excluded categories the influence of the proportion of unemployed adults was not significant and possibly reflects the lack of a clear dividing line between the concepts of "employed" and "unemployed" in the context of developing countries. This type of grey area is less likely in the case of physical capital.

Physical Capital

These assets contribute to household well-being both directly and indirectly. The less obvious or indirect benefits are captured in terms of, for example, time cost savings, market value and imputed value of rent. Some of these assets may also be used to generate income in own-account activities (Grootaert, Kanbur and Oh 1997). To begin, the housing quality variables are analysed before turning to the ownership of consumer durable variables. There may be theoretical objection to the inclusion of housing quality and household durables as variables in the regression on the grounds that they create problems of endogeneity. However, the motivation is different from that of the causes of poverty literature; the interest is in the factors that correlate with the well-being of households self-classified as poor and how this differs from the objective poor. Hence, these variables are important.

The main housing quality variables that are important correlates of consumption for both the subjective and objective poor are the *source of potable water* and *ownership of the land where households dwell*. Households that source their drinking water from stand pipes, wells, springs, ponds, rivers or rainwater consume significantly less than those who have water piped into their homes or on to their premises. The ownership of land has a positive – though not at all times significant – effect on household consumption. Here we must caution that the ownership of land is self-reported, with no proof of ownership required. For the pooled sample, in addition to the importance of the source of drinking water, the ownership of a telephone within the household had a positive and significant correlation with consumption, as seen in the 1999 and 1993 data. The *number of rooms* and the square of the number of rooms are also significant variables in 1993, but only the former is significant in the 1997 data. The data for 1993 show that with each additional room, consumption increased by 7.3 per cent, with a turning point occurring at the level of six rooms.

As in the case of housing conditions, the ownership of consumer durables influences household sense of well-being. The data suggest that ownership of consumer durables is generally associated with higher levels of consumption. The direction of influence and the variables that are significant bear a close similarity for the pooled sample and households self-classified as poor. In the pooled sample, all of the assets – with the exception of the ownership of a sewing machine – had a positive and significant influence on consumption in 1993. For the periods 1999 and 1997, ownership of a motor vehicle and gas stove is consistently associated with significant increases in consumption. Other significant variables suggested by the 1999 data, using the pooled sample, are ownership of a refrigerator and washing machine, while the 1997 data suggest that ownership of video equipment, stereo equipment and a radio cassette player is also important. The ownership of video equipment and a television is also a significant correlate of consumption for the subjective poor. The ownership of these assets may primarily be the result of household consumption rather than the converse, but it also influences household perception of their well-being, and, in this sense, ownership is important.

Relative to the pooled sample and the subjective poor, there is a notice-able difference in the number of assets that are important correlates of con-sumption of the objective poor and, in some cases, the direction of influence is counter-intuitive. Over the period of this study, the data show that owner-ship of a gas stove, radio cassette player, motor vehicle and television is asso-ciated with a positive influence on household consumption.[8] In 1999 and 1993 respectively, the ownership of a washing machine and stereo equip-ment were found to be associated with reduced levels of consumption. This result possibly reflects the reality of the different forms remittances take. It is very likely that these households would have received these items as gifts from friends or relatives living either in Jamaica or "a foreign" (living in a foreign country).

Conclusion

The results for the pooled sample and subjective poor suggest that male-headed households consume relatively more than female-headed households, and this is consistent with the literature that points to the likelihood of female-headed households being less well off. It has also been shown that subjectively poor single-female-headed households consume significantly more than other households. These results do not indicate the reasons why female-headed households consume less than male-headed households or the reasons some single-female-headed households consume more than other households, which are issues addressed in subsequent chapters.

There is clearly room for improvement in the average level of attendance of children at both primary and secondary school levels and, with the main reason for absence cited as money problems, it is not surprising that children are engaged in economic activities. Problems for households in educating their children, coupled with their involvement in child labour, expectedly influenced these households to classify themselves as poor. In fact, labour market activities of children may contribute to the difference in consumption between single-female-headed households others. It is also important to note that while the average number of children is larger in single-female-headed households relative to the pooled sample, it is below that of the objectively poor. Yet, in both the objective poor and the pooled sample, the influence of the child dependency ratio is consistent with expectations. There are a number of factors that influenced children's school attendance and household decisions to classify themselves as poor, which are taken up in chapters 6 and 7.

The influence of the elderly dependency ratio on consumption for the pooled sample and subjectively poor points to a general decline, which is the opposite of that for the objectively poor. These results point to the extended family structure, typical of developing countries, which possibly represents an important coping mechanism. The fact that the elderly in objectively poor households contribute positively to household consumption suggests that these individuals, in the absence of any serious ailment, go on working for as long as they can. The increasing number of elderly individuals in the population may also be an influence.

Educational attainment seems to be more important to the well-being of the objectively poor than the well-being of households who have classified themselves as poor. The proportion of unemployed adults had a negative influence on the consumption of subjectively poor households as well as all households in the pooled sample, but it did not affect the level of consumption of objectively poor households. The latter result possibly reflects strategies poor households employed in order to smooth consumption in the event of shocks.

For both subjectively and objectively poor households, housing quality variables and ownership of consumer durables significantly influence their well-being. The direction of influence of the variables was generally consistent with the results for the pooled sample, with greater consistency in the range of variables influencing the well-being of subjectively poor households and the pooled sample of all households.

Poverty in the context of Jamaica is not just about consumption, as issues of rights and justice (freedom from fear and protection of person and property), socio-economic and political participation; agency; and access to social services such as education, health, housing, water and sanitation must also be brought into the equation. While some of these factors are measurable and used in this book, the measurement of others is likely to pose a greater challenge but undoubtedly influences household perception of well-being. The subjective approach possibly allows some of these factors to be captured and reflected in the differences in the correlates of consumption for both objectively and subjectively poor households. It will be further unpacked in the next chapter which analyses the determinants of objective and subjective well-being.

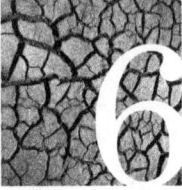

Determinants of Objective and Subjective Well-Being

This chapter compares the determinants of objective poverty with factors motivating households to classify themselves as poor, allowing the difference between objective and subjective approaches to poverty measurement to be established. The results suggest that the gender of the household head, educational attainment, dependants, household size and region of residence all influence household perception of well-being. These variables are also suggested by the literature and, in this book, as determinants of objective poverty. The results indicate that while the objective income poverty approach, based on household consumption, does not consider how the level of consumption was attained, households consider these conditions in the assessment of their well-being. These results have implications for programme participation and the indicators used to identify and target the poor since, in cases where households classified themselves as poor, they may also seek to register and participate in targeted programmes even though they are not "objectively poor".

The chapter is divided into four sections. The first outlines the methodology used in modelling poverty and a number of tests are conducted to determine whether the coefficients of the models should be pooled or not. The next section describes the determinants of poverty and household well-being. Objective and subjective approaches to poverty measurement are then compared so as to learn what might be different in the two approaches, followed by the conclusion.

Modelling the Probability of Being Poor

The probit model is used to establish the determinants of objective poverty and the likelihood of households classifying themselves as poor (including the marginal and impact effects on the probability of an event). Here the conditional probability ($0 < \Pr < 1$) of selecting a poor person (conditional on the coefficients and mean values of the explanatory variables) is written in the general form in which the underlying unobserved response variable y^* is defined by the following relationship:

$$y^* = \sum_{k=1}^{K} \beta_k x_k + \varepsilon \tag{6.1}$$

where β_k is the vector of parameters, x_k the vector of independent variables and ε_i the error term – assumed to be normally distributed – the probit model is therefore used. What is observed is a dummy variable y in equation 6.2:

$$y = \begin{cases} 1 & \textit{if } y^* > 0 \ (\textit{poor}) \\ 0 & \textit{non-poor} \end{cases} \tag{6.2}$$

The standardized cumulative normal distribution gives the probability of the event occurring for any value of y, where the probability is as follows:

$$\Pr(y = 1) = \Phi\left(\sum_{k=1}^{K} \beta_k x_k\right) \tag{6.3}$$

and the probability ($y = 0$) is equal to $1 - \Pr(y = 1)$.

Here $\Phi(\ )$ is the standard normal cumulative distribution function, x_k a vector of household characteristics and assets that influence the probability of the household being poor and β a vector of parameters to be estimated.

The objective is to establish differences or similarities in the contribution of assets and household characteristics to the likelihood that the households identify themselves as poor or their probability of being poor and thereby explaining what is different from subjective and objective poverty. Continuous variables are computed at the mean and calculated in equation 6.4:

$$\frac{\partial \Pr(y=1)}{\partial x_k} = \phi\left(\sum_{k=1}^{K}\beta_k x_k\right)\beta_k \qquad (6.4)$$

To arrive at the respective probabilities, the mean values (continuous variables) of assets and household characteristics are substituted into equation 6.4. This is to investigate the influence of assets, household demographics, socio-economic characteristics and geographic variables on the probability of being poor. The extent to which these probabilities differ will depend on the coefficients of the explanatory variables and the respective means.

To isolate the causes of poverty, some of the variables used in chapter 5 to model the correlates of consumption are excluded in analysing the objective determinants of poverty since they are not exogenous. As a result, some housing quality and all of the consumer durable variables which may influence household assessment of their own well-being are excluded because of their possible endogeneity – they are determined by the level of household consumption rather than the other way around. The influence of the determinants of poverty on the likelihood that households classify themselves as poor is also analysed. This permits the investigation of the mismatch in the variables between the objective determinants of poverty and factors influencing households to classify themselves as poor.

The influence of where the poverty line is set and the difference in scales on the determinants are also analysed. Strictly, for the purpose of sensitivity analysis, the original poverty threshold is adjusted upward by an average scale of one and one-third times, which is in accordance with the maximum minimum survival requirements suggested by all households. The results were generally consistent with the findings. The models of objective income poverty were also subjected to a number of tests of whether the coefficients of male-headed households and female-headed households or urban and rural areas should be pooled, and the results were generally significant in 1997. The test was also significant in 1999, having adjusted for scale, and this suggests that the determinants of consumption for urban and rural poor households are different. Similarly, tests for differences in the coefficients by gender of household head and region of residence were conducted when the objective poverty line was set based on the regional minimum survival requirements. In cases where the tests were significant, the appropriate disaggregated models are considered in the analysis.

Determinants of Poverty and Household Well-Being

In this section, the influence of (1) the gender and union status of the household head, (2) dependency ratios, (3) household size and (4) region of residence on the probability of being objectively poor on the likelihood households classify themselves as subjectively poor is analysed. Appropriate policy responses to the findings are also put forward. The analysis begins by looking at the gender of the household head.

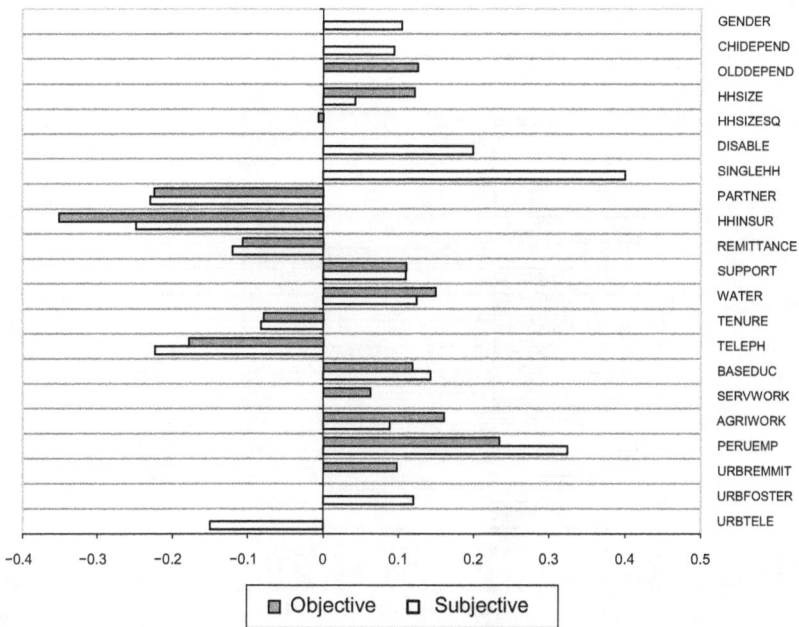

Figure 6.1a   Contribution of variables to the probability of being poor, 1999

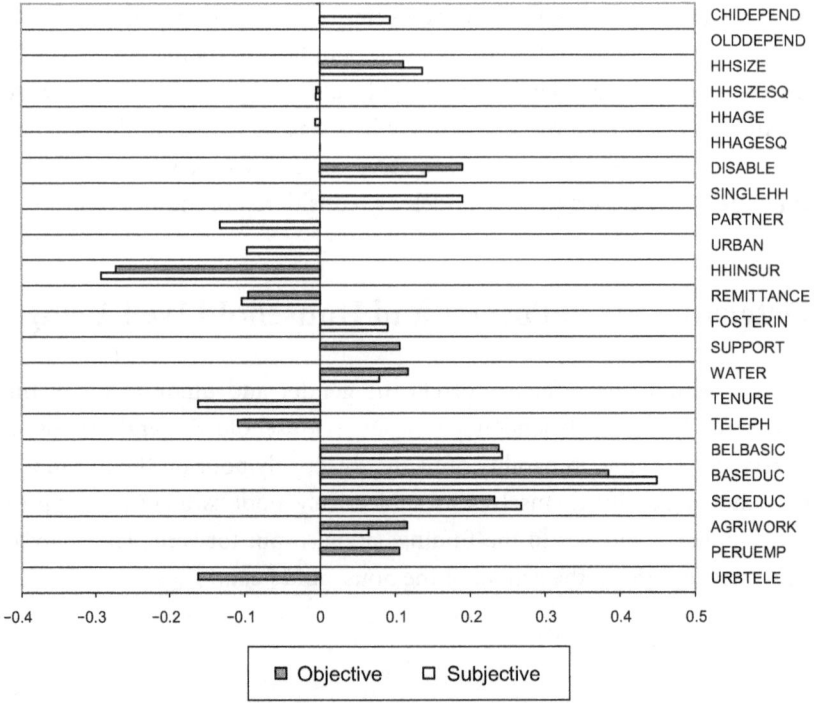

Figure 6.1b Contribution of variables to the probability of being poor, 1997

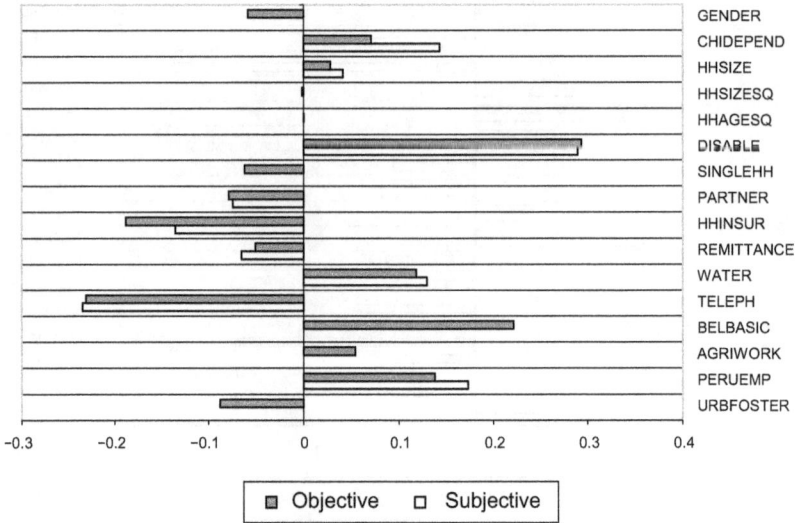

Figure 6.1c Contribution of variables to the probability of being poor, 1993

Table 6.1a   Probit Marginal and Impact Effects: The Probability of Being Poor, 1999

	(1)	(2)		(1)	(2)
GENDER	-0.049	0.105	TELEPH	-0.178	-0.223
	0.045	0.043*		0.048**	0.047**
CHIDEPEND	0.007	0.094	BASEDUC	0.119	0.143
	0.021	0.022**		0.055*	0.058*
OLDDEPEND	0.126	-0.040	SECEDUC	-0.008	0.077
	0.053*	0.052		0.058	0.061
HHSIZE	0.122	0.042	SERVWORK	0.063	0.026
	0.019**	0.019*		0.032*	0.032
HHSIZESQ	-0.006	-0.002	AGRIWORK	0.161	0.088
	0.002**	0.002		0.039**	0.038*
HHAGE	0.002	0.001	PERUEMP	0.234	0.324
	0.004	0.004		0.066**	0.073**
HHAGESQ	0.000	0.000	URBHINSU	0.131	-0.002
	0.000	0.000		0.106	0.100
DISABLE	0.080	0.199	URBREMIT	0.098	0.065
	0.082	0.079*		0.058+	0.059
SINGLEHH	-0.001	0.401	URBFOSTER	0.004	0.120
	0.048	0.046**		0.062	0.065+
PARTNER	-0.224	-0.229	URBSUPPT	0.016	0.057
	0.056**	0.055**		0.063	0.065
URBAN	-0.014	-0.050	URBWATER	0.075	0.058
	0.055	0.056		0.071	0.072
HHINSUR	-0.350	-0.248	URBTENURE	-0.013	0.001
	0.048**	0.054**		0.055	0.056
REMITTANCE	-0.106	-0.120	URBTELE	-0.097	-0.150
	0.037**	0.036**		0.069	0.072*
FOSTERIN	0.012	-0.006			
	0.046	0.044	Number of Obs.	1862	1862
SUPPORT	0.110	0.110	Log likelihood	-910.9	-886.0
	0.043*	0.042**	Wald (30)	508.5	453.5
WATER	0.150	0.124	Pseudo R2	0.285	0.304
	0.040**	0.039**	Correct Pred.	0.76	0.7
TENURE	-0.078	-0.082			
	0.040+	0.039*			

Notes: Models (1) and (2) reflect the subjective and objective poor respectively.

   [1]+, * and ** indicate significance at 10 per cent, 5 per cent and 1 per cent respectively.

   [2]Both the Pearson chi-square and Mosmer-Lemeshow goodness-of-fit tests suggest that the models fit reasonably well.

Gender of Head

The results of the probit models summarized in figures 6.1.a to 6.1.c and tables 6.1.a to 6.1.c suggest that the *gender of the household head* significantly influences the probability of being poor. This is somewhat different from the results of the mean income regressions, which show that although poor male-headed households consume more than female-headed households, the difference is not significant. Generally, the results of the probit

Table 6.1b   Probit Marginal and Impact Effects: The Probability of Being Poor, 1997

	(1)	(2)		(1)	(2)
GENDER	−0.045	0.039	BELBASED	0.238	0.242
	0.039	0.040		0.037**	0.022**
CHIDEPEND	0.010	0.093	BASICED	0.384	0.449
	0.022	0.029**		0.056**	0.056**
OLDDEPEND	0.039	−0.066	SECEDUC	0.232	0.268
	0.046	0.042		0.046**	0.044**
HHSIZE	0.111	0.136	SERVWORK	0.015	0.010
	0.016**	0.019**		0.027	0.027
HHSIZESQ	−0.005	−0.005	AGRIWORK	0.115	0.065
	0.001**	0.002**		0.034**	0.035+
HHAGE	−0.003	−0.006	PERUEMP	0.105	0.056
	0.003	0.003+		0.058+	0.062
HHAGESQ	0.000	0.000	URBHINSU	0.041	0.032
	0.000	0.000*		0.067	0.067
DISABLE	0.190	0.141	URBREMIT	0.009	0.003
	0.048**	0.051**		0.051	0.051
SINGLEHH	0.017	0.190	URBFOSTER	0.018	−0.106
	0.043	0.035**		0.060	0.080
PARTNER	−0.061	−0.132	URBSUPP	0.004	0.061
	0.061	0.062*		0.060	0.051
URBAN	−0.059	−0.097	URBWATER	0.072	0.077
	0.051	0.050+		0.060	0.057
HHINSUR	−0.272	−0.292	URBTENURE	0.050	0.071
	0.069**	0.070**		0.048	0.044
REMITTANCE	−0.095	−0.103	URBTELE	−0.162	−0.148
	0.040*	0.039**		0.063*	0.065*
FOSTERIN	−0.035	0.090			
	0.051	0.050+	Number of Obs.	1939	1939
SUPPORT	0.106	0.043	Log likelihood	−827.8	−774.4
	0.041**	0.040	Wald (29)	471.3	563.1
WATER	0.116	0.079	Pseudo R2	0.326	0.373
	0.035**	0.035*	Correct Pred.	0.8	0.81
TENURE	−0.058	−0.161			
	0.039	0.038**			
TELEPH	−0.109	−0.114			
	0.049*	0.051*			

Notes: (1) Models 1 and 2 reflect the subjective and objective poor respectively;

(2) +, * and ** indicate significance at 10 per cent, 5 per cent and 1 per cent respectively.

models, though not consistent, suggest that male-headed households are significantly less likely to be poor relative to female-headed households. These households were 5.8 per cent less likely to be poor in 1993, but in the absence of adjustment for scales, the signs of the coefficients, although consistent with the results, are not significant. The results of the disaggregated 1997 data by region suggest that for households residing in urban and rural regions, male-headed households are less likely to be poor. These results, although consistent, were also not significant at a conventional level.

Table 6.1c   Probit Marginal and Impact Effects: The Probability of Being Poor, 1993

	(1)	(2)		(1)	(2)
GENDER	−0.058	−0.006	BELBASED	0.221	0.158
	0.025*	0.025		0.128+	0.121
CHIDEPEND	0.071	0.144	BASICED	0.082	0.038
	0.015**	0.016**		0.052	0.055
OLDDEPEND	−0.022	−0.031	SECEDUC	0.093	0.050
	0.032	0.033		0.066	0.064
HHSIZE	0.028	0.042	SERVWORK	−0.017	−0.002
	0.012*	0.013**		0.023	0.023
HHSIZESQ	−0.002	−0.001	AGRIWORK	0.054	0.044
	0.001+	0.001		0.028+	0.029
HHAGE	−0.003	0.000	PERUEMP	0.138	0.173
	0.004	0.004		0.043**	0.042**
HHAGESQ	0.000	0.000	URBHINSU	0.009	−0.098
	0.000*	0.000		0.126	0.075
DISABLE	0.293	0.289	URBREMIT	−0.013	0.009
	0.083**	0.082**		0.044	0.046
SINGLEHH	−0.062	0.034	URBFOSTER	−0.088	−0.074
	0.028*	0.034		0.037*	0.039+
PARTNER	−0.079	−0.074	URBSUPP	0.071	0.052
	0.023**	0.023**		0.059	0.057
URBAN	0.018	0.046	URBWATER	0.065	0.060
	0.064	0.064		0.050	0.052
HHINSUR	−0.188	−0.135	URBTENURE	−0.016	−0.045
	0.042**	0.052**		0.059	0.060
REMITTANCE	−0.050	−0.065	URBTELE	0.019	0.078
	0.027+	0.027*		0.116	0.130
FOSTERIN	0.031	0.001			
	0.037	0.034	Number of Obs.	1910	1910
SUPPORT	0.010	0.034	Log likelihood	−867.5	−796.5
	0.031	0.033	Wald (31)	349.8	431.8
WATER	0.119	0.130	Pseudo R2	0.236	0.298
	0.031**	0.032**	Correct Pred.	0.77	0.79
TENURE	−0.023	−0.003			
	0.050	0.050			
TELEPH	−0.231	−0.234			
	0.039**	0.036**			

Notes: (1) Models 1 and 2 reflect the subjective and objective poor respectively;

(2) +, * and ** indicate significance at 10 per cent, 5 per cent and 1 per cent respectively.

Given the relative educational attainment of male and female household heads, and the greater likelihood of boys dropping out of school (also reflected in lower enrolment rates at the university level), the reduced likelihood of male-headed households being poor is not quite clear. It may, however, be related to their industry of employment and/or occupation; the higher labour force participation rate for males, averaging approximately 49 per cent during the 1990s; unobserved labour market distortions;[1] and the higher incidence of self-reported, ill-health by women

(Handa and Neitzert 1998). Some of these factors may also influence the perception, on behalf of single-female-headed households,[2] of their well-being.

The data also point to interesting contrasts between objective poverty and household perception of their well-being. While male-headed households were less likely to be objectively poor, they were also more likely to classify themselves as subjectively poor. The variable *gender* was significant only in 1999, which suggests that male-headed households were 10.5 per cent more likely to classify themselves as subjectively poor relative to female-headed households. In addition, controlling for the objectively poor in the models used to estimate subjective poverty, the likelihood of male-headed households classifying themselves as poor became significant for the period under review. The reasons these households classify themselves as poor will be explored, but first the fact that the results for male-headed households are no different from those for single-female-headed households will be highlighted. Single-female-headed households were 6.2 per cent less likely to be objectively poor in 1993, yet they are generally more likely to classify themselves as subjectively poor. The probability of classifying themselves as subjectively poor is even greater once objective poverty is controlled for. In this light, targeting policies that generally see female-headed households as a disadvantaged group may result in considerable leakage to the non-poor and less than desirable coverage of the objective poor.

Explanations for the reasons male-headed households and single-female-headed households are less likely to be objectively poor but at the same time more likely to classify themselves as subjectively poor are put forward. In analysing the above findings, the relative levels of female and male educational attainment, instrumented by the relative proportion graduating from the University of the West Indies, Mona campus, are analysed. This provides the background against which the data on occupation, employment, earnings, consumption and perception of well-being should be understood.

According to the literature, at all levels of the tertiary educational system in Jamaica, females outperform males (both in terms of enrolment and certification). However, males seem to do better in the technical, vocational, and pure and applied science fields at the post-secondary level. Nonetheless, in 1998 more women graduated from each department and within each class of degree from the University of the West Indies, varying between 83 per cent of individuals with upper second and 58 per cent of individuals with pass degrees. This possibly reflects the fact that 74 per cent of graduates were female (PIOJ 2000), compared with 51 per cent registered in 1982. It seems that females take advantage of educational opportunities and outperform males, but this may not have translated into higher social status and earnings. One explanation for the greater number of women with tertiary education may be that the returns to education for women are greater than for men, but further research is needed to establish this notion. Women with better educational outcomes may have higher expected levels of well-being, and if these expected levels are unmet, they are likely to perceive their well-being as lower than it actually is. This may be one of the factors contributing to the likelihood of female-headed households (in particular single-female-headed households) classifying themselves as poor.[3] Does this also suggest that better educated women choose to remain single? Clearly further research is needed to explore the relationship between education and single-female-headed households. Interestingly, the data in table 6.2 show that single-female-headed households with better educational outcomes are more likely to classify themselves as subjectively poor than male-headed households with the same educational outcomes.

Unlike single-female-headed households, those male-headed households classifying themselves as subjectively poor have lower academic achievement in terms both of examinations passed and of average years of schooling. Their mean consumption expenditure is also the lowest among subjectively poor households. Table 6.2 also suggests that while women are outperforming men and subjectively poor single-female-headed households have better educational outcomes (75 per cent of households classified as only subjectively poor, who possess A-level qualifications or more, are single-female-headed households), in general, more than half the household heads with CXC passes, GCE passes and further educational qualifications are male-headed households. It seems that part of the reason some male-headed households are classifying themselves as poor is due to the fact that they have lower educational outcomes relative to the general situation for both male-headed households and female-headed households. This is also translated into lower levels of consumption expenditure. In other words, while they are above the objective poverty threshold, they are relatively less well off, and hence there is the tendency to classify themselves as poor. Clearly, the issue to be addressed is the reason some female-headed households are classifying

Table 6.2   Distribution of Educational Achievement of Head, 1999

Examination Passed by Household Head	All Households		Subjectively Poor		Only Subjectively Poor	
	MHHs	SFHHs	MHHs	SFHHs	MHHs	SFHHs
None	62.5	24.9	53.4	36.6	49.4	50.6
CXC and GCE	54.1	33.8	44.4	55.6	44.4	55.6
A levels +	60.3	29.4	28.6	71.4	25.0	75.0
Average years of education of head	7.8	7.7	7.0	7.6	7.5	7.7
*Average years of education of spouse	5.4	4.6	4.5	4.4	2.7	2.6

Note: *Data refer to education of spouse of male-headed households and female-headed households.
Source: PIOJ, JSLC 1999 data set.

themselves as poor when their educational achievement is better than their male counterparts.

Part of the explanation for the difference in well-being between male-headed households and female-headed households and the tendency for single-female-headed households to classify themselves as poor may lie in the occupational choices and/or opportunities of men and women. Over the period 1990–1998, males were predominantly in occupations as *self-employed and independent craftsmen,* and *plant and machine operations and assemblers.* Males were also employed in *production process and operations, unskilled manual and general/craft and related trades,* and in *skilled agriculture* and *fishery* occupations. Women dominated the following groups: *professional, technical, administrative, executive and managerial,* as well as working as *clerks and service workers,* in *shop and market sales* and as *domestic helpers* (Ricketts and Benfield 2000; PIOJ 2001).

This general trend is also seen in table 6.3, among household heads using the 1999 data, and it is much more evident among households classified as subjectively poor. Of household heads in the occupational groups Professionals, Clerks and Sales and Elementary Occupations, over half of those classified as subjectively poor are single-female-headed households, while a greater proportion of heads in Skill Agriculture and Fisheries, Craft and Related Trades, and Plant and Machine Operators classified as

Table 6.3   Distribution of Occupational Groups of Head, 1999

Occupational Groups	All Households		Subjectively Poor		Only Subjectively Poor	
	MHHs	SFHHs	MHHs	SFHHs	MHHs	SFHHs
Professionals	56.6	31.9	42.9	51.0	22.2	77.8
Clerks & sales	42.0	38.4	28.6	66.2	37.0	63.0
Elementary occupations	41.8	41.1	30.7	51.5	25.9	74.1
Skill agriculture & fisheries	77.9	14.8	73.0	21.5	72.2	27.8
Craft & related trades	74.8	13.7	64.4	26.7	66.7	33.3
Plant & machine operators	72.6	13.2	52.2	43.5	50.0	50.0

Source: PIOJ 1999.

subjectively poor are male-headed households. These results seem to point to some level of occupational sex segregation, but this conclusion is reserved so as to take the time to look at the sector and industry of employment of the head/principal earner of households.

An examination of the sector of employment based on the 1999 data suggests that a larger proportion of male-headed households are in the private sector, are employers, and are in own-account work, and a similar proportion of male-headed households and female-headed households are employed in the local or central government and other government agencies. This suggests that the proportion of women in the public sector was greater than their overall proportion relative to men and is consistent with aggregate data, reported by the Economic and Social Survey of Jamaica (PIOJ 2001), which shows that women accounted for 53.8 per cent of public sector employees.[4] Most of the male-headed households classified as subjectively poor are in *own-account* activities (65.8 per cent), while subjectively poor single-female-headed households predominate in the private sector (45.0 per cent) and *own-account* (45.5 per cent) activities. Given the large proportion of subjectively poor male-headed households in the informal sector, the perception of their well-being may also be influenced by greater instability experienced in their earnings.

Table 6.4   Distribution of Poor Households by Industrial Classification, 1999

Head of HH	1	2	3	4	5	6	7	8	9
MHHs	26.0	74.1	67.7	32.1	24.4	57.1	40.0	53.3	74.1
SFHHs	44.2	17.9	19.4	35.7	48.9	28.6	50.0	33.3	14.8
Head count	13.9	29.2	10.1	13.2	17.1	4.5	4.7	4.3	8.8
Adjustment for Scales									
MHHs	32.9	75.4	64.0	30.8	31.3	65.4	51.1	50.8	74.4
SFHHs	44.3	17.3	21.0	41.8	48.7	23.1	35.6	34.3	13.3
Head count	41.1	67.7	32.7	42.9	43.7	16.6	21.1	19.1	29.4

Note: (1) Service workers; (2) agricultural workers; (3) mining, manufacturing and construction; (4) wholesale and retail services; (5) restaurant and hotel services, amusement, and
personal and domestic services; (6) transport, storage, communications and financial
services; (7) government service, private medical practice and professional associations;
(8) government officials, managers, senior officials and professionals; (9) builders,
machine operators, textile, food and wood products.
Source: PIOJ 1999.

Analysis of the pattern of labour market participation of the principal
earner of poor households suggests that poor male heads are overly represented in the Agriculture, Manufacturing, Mining and Construction, Transport, Storage, Communications and Financial Services, and Builders and
Machine Operators industries, but these proportions are generally below
their national averages. At the same time, the proportion of poor females in
these industries is above their national proportion and is also seen generally
for all industries nationally (see table 6.4). This clearly points to the case of
vertical occupational segregation since females are overly represented at the
lower end of the occupational scales and are likely to be least protected, so
that the fact that difference between consumption in male-headed households and female-headed households was not significant masked other gender inequalities and instead reflects the many support mechanisms used by
females.

There is also the unsubstantiated notion that unlike women, men are
reluctant to take up low-paying jobs and may prefer to get involved in petty
trading and other risky or illegal activities, while women seek to complement their income by adopting several coping strategies. Hidden behind

the results, therefore, is the general belief that although there is no significant difference in consumption between poor male-headed households and
female-headed households, the latter may have attained their well-being
through greater effort, and this may also influence single-female-headed
households' perception of their well-being.[5]

The results suggest that there is occupational and industrial segregation
by gender, but the literature on Jamaica focuses on the former. The literature
is not conclusive about the degree of occupational segregation[6] (Hotchkiss
and Moore [1996] reporting a Duncan Index of 9 per cent, while Handa
and Neitzert [1998] only acknowledge that it exists, and Olsen and Coppin
[2001] see it as part of the colonial legacy), and given the limitations of the
Duncan Index,[7] the general consensus is that male and female occupational
stereotyping/segregation does exist and is possibly an important source
of compensation disparity (for other limitations of the Duncan Index, see
Preston 1999, 613–14). Although it is established that women predominate
in low-paying jobs, there is a notable and increasing proportion of women
in middle management positions, especially in the government sector. As
indicated above, subjectively poor single-female-headed households outnumber male-headed households in the top occupational groups of Professionals, Senior Officials and Technicians. Nonetheless, a glass ceiling seems
to exist, obstructing the path of upwardly mobile women, compounded
by the fact that their experience may not be rewarded commensurate with
their male counterparts. In fact, according to the Jamaica Human Development Report (PIOJ 2000), women occupy 10 per cent of the senior jobs
in the private and public sectors. This is evident in the small number of
females on the boards of companies (8 per cent of board members of all
publicly listed companies were women), and where they are found in the
top occupational group, they still do not command positions at the highest
levels, even when similarly experienced to their male counterparts (Ricketts and Benfield 2000). In fact, Hotchkiss and Moore (1996) argue that
women earn less than men at every age, and the disparity is slightly greater
for older workers. This resonates somewhat with Scott's (1992, 323) findings that in Jamaica, women's weekly earnings in 1989 were 57.7 per cent
of men's earnings. Hotchkiss and Moore (1996) also state that "the mean
salary of women in formal sector employment is 80.0 per cent of the mean
salary for men".[8] Similarly, Bailey and Ricketts (2003, 60) argue that wage
disparities that favour men exist at both the lowest and highest ends of

the wage scale, while James and Williams (2003) show that males earned between 10 per cent and 55 per cent more than females during the 1990s.

The data also suggest that while more women have entered the labour force in recent times and have higher levels of education, they experience higher levels of unemployment than men – averaging 22.6 per cent compared with 10.1 per cent for men during the period 1990–1998. The data for 1999 show that, of those households whose head is unemployed, 51.0 per cent are female-headed households, and single-female-headed households account for 67.6 per cent of unemployed female-headed households. Using the merged JSLC and Jamaica Labour Force Survey data, the distribution of unemployed heads of households classified as subjectively poor shows that the proportion of unemployed female-headed households increased from 45.5 per cent in 1993 to 60.5 per cent in 1999. Over the period, the proportion of single-female-headed households among unemployed, subjectively poor households increased from 10 per cent to 48.3 per cent (see figure 6.2). In addition, while females accounted for 42.7 per cent of the labour force in 1999, most persons in the employed labour force who do not possess any training or possessing vocational training but no certification are males. These findings lend support to the statistical discrimination theory (Anker 1997), and it is therefore of no surprise that female-headed households are predominant among the group of households classifying themselves as subjectively poor. The findings are also consistent with the literature that points to the importance of employment in household perception of their well-being.

Established above is the fact that single-female-headed households are less likely than male-headed households to be objectively poor. Nonetheless, single-female-headed households are generally more likely to

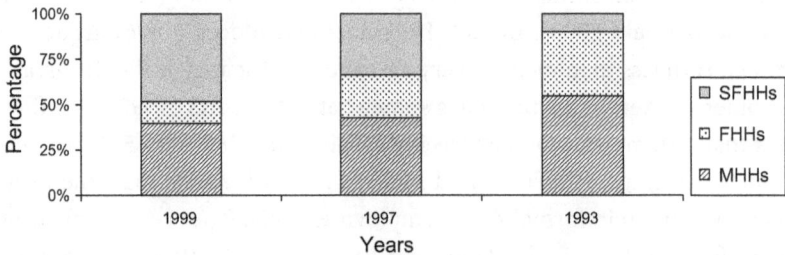

Figure 6.2 Distribution of unemployed subjectively poor households

identify themselves as poor, and this is clearly related to their vulnerability or likelihood of becoming poor. It is also likely that if single-female-headed households' well-being is less stable and they experience greater spells of poverty at any given time, they will be more likely to classify themselves as poor. Further research is therefore needed to establish the extent to which female-headed households experience greater spells of poverty and how the situation of single-female-headed households is compared with that of other households. This is particularly important since, among households classified as only subjectively poor, just over half of the households with no qualifications are single-female-headed households.

Their greater vulnerability and possibly greater spells of poverty are related not only to the fact that single-female-headed households are generally equally represented among household heads with lower educational outcomes, but also to labour market distortions. This is supported by results suggesting that women still predominate in low-paying occupations, and they are overly represented at the lower end of the scale. In addition, using the 2001 population census data, Ricketts (2005) argues that the mean wages of females is below the average for males at every level of examination passed. Even in professions such as teaching and nursing – professions that are predominantly filled by women – salaries are relatively low, but these occupational choices, according to the human capital model, may reflect the trade-off between household responsibilities, labour market demands and the need for job security (employer preferences may also be relevant). This may also be influenced by the inability of the household to depend on a second person as a stable source of income. This implies that single-female-headed households may need to work continuously simply to earn a living, and this should translate into greater labour market experience and the type of occupational choices made, but they may still see themselves as vulnerable.

The vulnerability of these households seems to be related to a combination of factors, such as low human capital, high reliance on family and friends for financial support, social safety net programmes, labour market distortions and household responsibilities. And household responsibilities have implications for the choice of job. It therefore seems that policies which make these households less reliant on the sources of family are needed, and perhaps this may be achieved through appropriate education and measures that eliminate labour market distortions.

This section has illustrated that despite women's educational attainment relative to men, they are still underrepresented in the top positions of companies. Women are concentrated in stereotypical occupations and industries, and are overly represented at the lower ends of the occupational scales. These conditions exist due to a number of factors identified, all of which influence the perception by female-headed households of their well-being. Policies that promote training for women and men in non-traditional occupations, foster the removal of occupational segregation, remove gender stereotypes and prejudice, and help women and families to combine work and child care/housework responsibilities, may prove important in informing the sense of well-being for female-headed households. Equally important are initiatives that encourage boys to stay in school, which may have long-term effects on earnings and male-headed households' perception of their well-being.[9] The next section analyses the influence of the dependency ratios on the probability of being poor as well as household sense of well-being.

Dependency Ratios

Child Dependants

The literature on child-bearing sees children as "durable consumer goods", "old age security" and, in some countries, "producer goods". This suggests that, in some cases, children contribute positively to the current well-being of households, and the direction of influence of the *child dependency ratio* on the probability of being poor need not conform to the general expectation of an increase. This is seen in the analysis of the effect of the variable on the consumption of objectively and subjectively poor households. The inconsistency is further apparent in the effect of the variable on the probability of being objectively poor and household self-assessment of their well-being. A one-unit increase in the *child dependency ratio* leads to increased probability of being poor and the likelihood that some households classify themselves as subjectively poor. The influence of child dependency ratio on the likelihood that households classify themselves as poor remains significant, even after controlling for the influence of the objectively poor. This indicates consistency in the results of the mean income regression and the probit models.

As established, these households may have achieved their well-being status by involving their children in economic activities and exposing them to possible exploitation (Ennew and Young [1981] catalogue a number of income-earning activities in which children are involved) at the expense of their education.[10] This result suggests that while the literature on child dependency continues to be relevant primarily for poor households and for children below a certain age, the growing involvement of children in economic activities is of policy concern and clearly influences the household's perception and expectation of its well-being.[11]

The concern for child dependency is related to its impact on household resources and the burden placed on employed individuals in poor households. This relationship is supported by this work. To the extent that child employment is closely related to adult unemployment and unmet basic needs, as suggested in the literature, it is not surprising that these households classify themselves as poor. The data suggest that the proportion of unemployed adults to those employed was greatest for subjectively poor households, with the proportion being even higher for single-female-headed households, at 15.6 per cent. Policies geared towards the reduction of poverty must therefore pursue initiatives that seek to keep children in school[12] and, at the same time, improve the income-earning potential of the household. These issues will be addressed at a later stage in this chapter.

Also of policy interest are the characteristics of the children involved in child labour and the actual prevalence of the practice. While the former are assessed based on the birth ordering and gender of children, the latter cannot accurately be estimated from the survey and instead the literature must be relied upon.[13] In the 1999 JSLC survey, households were asked, "Do you ever stop your child from going to school because of financial difficulties?" For 33.6 per cent of the children (34.6 per cent of households), the response was affirmative, with a median of three days for the first and second child, and five days for the third child. There is no indication as to whether the ordering of the children relates to their age; however, 89 per cent of the children not sent to school were from the group "first child". The data suggest that boys account for 60.3 per cent of the first-child group, while 53.1 per cent and 56.3 per cent of the second- and third-child groups are girls.

If the ordering of the children is related to their age, then the birth order of the child also influences child labour, and boys seem to be more involved in this practice.

How prevalent is the practice of child labour? The World Bank (cited by Ennew and Young 1981) estimated that one in every thousand Jamaican children was involved in the labour force, and this was predicted to drop to 0.2 per thousand by 2000. The estimate is in stark contrast to the findings of Ennew and Young (1981). Their estimate is 11.6 per thousand from a sample of 2,146 children, six to eighteen years old in 1980, and this does not consider children who do not attend school at all, perform part-time and holiday work, or who are involved in informal apprenticeships. If the estimates based on Ennew and Young's study are still relevant, they are quite significant, considering that approximately 32.8 per cent of the total population was less than fourteen years of age in 2000. This translates into approximately 10,000 children involved in child labour, which, at best, is a very conservative estimate and is in stark contrast to unofficial estimates of 20,000 for 1997. Estimates for 2002, based on a child activity survey conducted by the Statistical Agency of Jamaica, suggest that 2.2 per cent of children aged five to seventeen years, meaning 16240 children, were involved in economic activities. Just over three quarters of these children were boys.

Elderly Dependants

As with the *child dependency ratio*, the direction of influence of the *elderly dependency ratio* is not consistent. The results of the probit models show that the probability of being objectively poor decreased by an average of 3.8 per cent for 1997 and 1993. After adjusting for scale, the latter results are inconsistent with results, suggesting significant increases in the probability of being poor by 12.6 per cent in 1999. There is a reversal in the sign of the coefficients for the other years, suggesting a decrease in the probability of being poor, but the results are not significant. This suggests that the contributions of elderly individuals in poor households are not at all times greater than their claims on household spending.[14] As previously argued, this result indicates the poor cannot afford to stop working at the retirement age, but it may also be motivated by the larger proportion of the elderly in the population and the recognition that these individuals can go on to contribute positively after the retirement age.[15] In fact, among objectively poor households, there is a tendency – shown in chapter 7 – for poor households to incorrectly classify themselves as not poor because of the positive contribution of the elderly to these households.

Controlling for objectively poor households in the models used to estimate subjective poverty, the *elderly dependant ratio* was at no point significant but generally suggested a reduction in the likelihood that these households classify themselves as poor. However, in 1993, the coefficient changed from negative to positive after controlling for the objectively poor. These results suggest that while some households are classifying themselves as poor because of the need to support elderly members, there are some households whose elderly members contribute positively to household well-being, reducing the likelihood that the household classifies itself as poor. The extent to which this fact impacts the likelihood of objectively poor households with elderly members contributing positively to their well-being incorrectly classifying themselves as not poor is not clear. The former scenario may result, however, if elderly members in these households have withdrawn from the labour market, are not in receipt of pensions or the amount received is substantially lower than average, or did not make adequate provision for their old age, and, as such, are net users of resources when compared to the situation in poor households.

Saddled with the responsibility of taking care of the elderly, which can be expensive if health care and medication-related costs are included, households can perceive their well-being as lower than it is based on the objective poverty threshold. This may be related to the fact that their actual average consumption is below their expected attainable well-being and may be formed by the outlays made in support of family members – the deserving elderly – and the likelihood that elderly members in other households may not appear to be as dependant.[16]

Unlike the situation with child dependants, elderly dependants exert a downward influence on the amount of resources available to each member, which supports Lipton and Ravallion's (1995) argument that the age structure of poor households implies high dependency ratios. These high dependence ratios can be a drag on the overall participation in work and current sense of well-being. This position is not conclusively supported in the case of Jamaica since both children and the elderly participate in the labour market. Lipton and Ravallion (1995) also recognize that the high dependency ratio increases the marginal utility of income-per-worker relative to leisure, and the average participation rate is therefore invariably raised through the employment of children and the elderly. This position is further supported by Ennew and Young's (1981) argument that one of the survival strategies of poor households in Jamaica is to ensure that all possible household members obtain an income. An interesting contrast emerges here: in poor households, the elderly are working beyond retirement age, making a positive contribution to consumption, and children are net users of household's resources. In households self-classified as poor, however, the converse occurs. Is it the case that some households invest in the future of their children while others mortgage their future? It is not possible to answer this question, but further research looking at the intergenerational transmission of poverty and the mechanisms through which it is transferred is needed.

The findings show that, consistent with the literature on *child dependency ratio*, a one-unit increase in this variable leads to increased probability of being objectively poor. Similarly, the effect of the *child dependency ratio* on the likelihood of households classifying themselves as poor is the same as for the objectively poor. For the *elderly dependency ratio*, a one-unit increase leads to increased consumption for objectively poor households, but for households self-classified as poor, the direction of influence of the *elderly dependency ratio* was the opposite in 1993. Viewed together, the results for households self-classified as poor suggest that they may be caught in a low-level consumption trap in which children are likely to be underachievers and may not secure a "good" job, thus involving the second generation of children in activities to support the household consumption. As Basu and Tzannatos (2003) argue, a child labourer tends to grow up to have children who are child labourers by virtue of their family history.[17] This is consistent with Baland and Robinson's (1998) notion of the impossibility of intergenerational contracting and represents a mechanism for the transfer of income from children to parents. Coupled with the possible dependency of their parents – the elderly – who may not be in receipt of a pension, their expected future well-being may be too uncertain for the households to classify themselves other than poor. Equally important to the decision of these households to classify themselves as poor may be the social stigma cost of sending their children out to work (Basu and Tzannatos 2003; Grootaert and Kanbur 1995). The following analysis seeks to address issues relating to the appropriate response to child labour.

Policy Implications

One segment of the literature suggests that the problem of child labour may be addressed by measures that reduce children's labour market activities and improve school attendance. The economic activities in which children are engaged are, however, diverse, and children are involved for different reasons and under varying conditions. There are street children who are abused and sexually exploited as well as other working children, and these groups may not be mutually exclusive. There are several remedial programmes in Jamaica but the focus seems to be on children who have dropped out of school, street children, those at risk and those involved in prostitution (PIOJ 2001). While it is recognized that there are some children whose school attendance may be affected by their labour market activities, many of the initiatives such as the School Lunch Programme, the PATH[18] and the Cost-Sharing Scheme, geared towards encouraging attendance, may be misguided since, in some cases, the necessary research has not been done.

Invariably, the focus of these programmes is on the needs of the child rather than those of the household, and, consequently, drop-out rates remain high and attendance levels continue to be low for some children. These problems will continue if there is a failure to recognize that the decision about whether to send children to school or not is influenced by the care giver whose choice may be seen in terms of constraints, incentives and agency (Bhalotra 2003). As a result, if the constraint that pushed children into work is poverty, the policy response may generally seek to provide the household with a cash transfer (Ravallion and Wodon 2000). An evaluation by the author of the pilot phase of the PATH raises questions about this approach. It revealed that households received the benefit, but there was no discernable improvement in children's level of school attendance. The reason identified by the respondents was the inadequate amounts received relative to the costs of schooling for their children. This suggests that the success of this approach clearly depends on the income effect and parents' altruism,[19] where it is assumed that there is a negative effect of parental income on child labour. As established, some of these households may not be consumption poor; this is consistent with studies that show the poverty effect on child labour to be small (Bhalotra 2003; Bhalotra and Tzannatos 2002; Grootaert 1998; Kassouf 1998; Psacharopoulos 1997). In other cases, such as the study by Ray (1999), a positive relationship between poverty and child labour was not found in Peru. These results are clearly possible, as demonstrated in this book, since the minimum acceptable income that the household sees as necessary may not coincide with the established income poverty threshold. Therefore, the use of the headcount based on income poverty lines may not explain child labour (Basu and Tzannatos 2003), yet these households may perceive themselves as poor. Consistent with the latter argument, Bhalotra and Heady (2003), using data for Ghana and Pakistan, show that households that own larger plots of land tend to work their children more (they recognize also that households that send their children to work for wages are poorer on average), so a greater likelihood of being poor may not lead to increased child labour. The results for Ghana and Pakistan are, nonetheless, somewhat different from my findings, because those households whose children are more likely to engage in child labour are not objectively poor but are likely to classify themselves as poor, and the income effect of a given transfer may not be as large as for households who are objectively poor.

Nonetheless, school attendance is influenced not only by the amount of resources at the disposal of the household but also by parent interest in educating their children. In situations where parent interest may not coincide with that of the child's, as suggested in focus group meetings, legislature that prohibits child labour or makes schooling compulsory may prove effective in raising the level of attendance. School attendance may also be affected if the cost of schooling is too high, inaccessible or of poor quality.[20] In these situations, even if the household is not poor, a rational decision may be made to send the child to work, especially if experience gained is valuable in the labour market. This may explain why some boys miss school. In this scenario, the reward for working exceeds the rewards of schooling, and policies that make schooling more attractive are likely to reduce child labour (Grootaert and Kanbur 1995; Psacharopoulos 1997; Ravallion and Wodon 2000).

In reality, as suggested in chapter 5, many children combine work and school, and this may be common when children work on family farms or enterprises, allowing them to attend school when their labour is not needed. The literature suggests that in these cases, when work does not interfere with children's education (including time spent reading and doing home work) it allows them to develop skills that are advantageous to them as adults and broadens their future opportunities (Satz 2003).[21] In this case, policies that promote school attendance may be more successful than those that discourage child labour, such as legislation against the practice (Basu and Tzannatos 2003) or minimum wages that remove the need for children to work. Within the context of the findings, a reduction in child labour may also necessitate the provision of income support to the elderly in these households and is consistent with findings in Brazil and England. Another strategy through which school attendance may be enhanced is by the removal of supply-side constraints, such as lack of capacity at the secondary level and improved quality of education. The solution may also require that the conditions (with attention paid to the gender of the child) of each household be addressed on their own merits with attempts made to inform parents of the cost of child labour and the possible medium and long-term benefits of education. Providing them with information would allow them to make more informed decisions. Equally important is the need for further research that isolates the key determinants of child labour so that appropriate policies may be put forward. Both of these initiatives, however, are beyond the scope of this book.

This section addressed the importance of household composition and the contribution of household members to well-being and how this informs both the probability of being poor and household perception of their well-being. The following sections examine the role of household size and location of residence in the probability of being poor and household likelihood of classifying themselves as poor.

Household Size

Household size and the square of this variable are generally significant both as determinants of objective poverty and households classifying themselves as subjectively poor. A one-unit increase in *household size* increases the probability of being poor by an average of 2.3 per cent, in the absence of adjustment for scales, but the negative sign on the variable *square of household size* suggests that this effect will increase up to a point before declining. The turning points occurred at fifteen and nine household members in 1999 and 1993 respectively. With adjustment for scales, the average poverty increasing effect is 9.1 per cent and the turning point varied between ten and thirteen household members. These results may be influenced by the relationship between household size, the dependency ratio (the correlation between household size and child dependency ratio is 0.47) and the type of family structure prevalent in Jamaica where household members may be related through different types of lineage relationships, which may also be seen as a coping/livelihoods strategy.

In order to examine the effect the type of family structure has on the probability of being poor, this variable is instrumented using the relationship of the child(ren) to the household head for those households (93.9 per cent) who received child support in 1999. Relative to the comparison category – *households whose head is not related to the child* – those whose head is a *grandparent* or the *biological parent* are less likely to be poor, while households whose head is a *relative* are more likely to be poor. Only the result for *grandparents* was significant in 1999, while the results for 1997 indicate that, unlike the other variables, there is a reversal in the sign of the coefficient for *biological parents*. This result also suggests that there may be various types of extended family arrangements, or siblings and their families living together, adapting various sharing arrangements. This may be particularly evident in rural areas and inner city communities in Kingston, where individuals are employed in seasonal activities. The general reading of these results suggests that for the poor, the composition of the household is as important as its size. This scenario implies that *household size* may not be endogenous but rather the sharing arrangements that evolve. How to disentangle one from the other is not clear, and the adjustment for economies of scale may mean some of the factors that motivate household sharing arrangements have been isolated.

Although the sample is limited to households in receipt of child support, the results suggest that a sizeable proportion of households have children who are not directly related to the head. In these cases, the majority of heads are a grandparent, of which 44.3 per cent are single-female-headed households; this accounts for 58.6 per cent of grandparents reporting being poor and 43.4 per cent estimated as objectively poor. Most grandparents (84.6 per cent) who have classified themselves as poor are single-female-headed households. To the extent that these households are caring for their second generation – for which they may not be appropriately compensated – they are likely to see themselves as poorer than they actually are, and it is therefore of no surprise that household size also influences household perception of their well-being status. The average poverty-increasing effect is 7.3 per cent, with turning points varying between eleven and twenty-two household members.

Household size and the square of this variable remained generally significant determinants of households classifying themselves as poor, when controlling for objectively poor households. *Household size* was not significant in 1999, but the sign on the coefficient is positive, and the opposite of the sign on square household size. The results for 1997 and 1993 are significant and consistent with those for 1999, suggesting an increase in the likelihood that households classified themselves as poor. It may be that factors such as overcrowding, coupled with the number of dependants and female-headed households, may lead these households to perceive their well-being to be lower than it actually is and classify themselves as poor. This result implies that policies that result in smaller household size or reduced levels of dependency are consistent with reduced likelihood of being poor and improved household perception of well-being. Concerning a strategy to tackle this, the literature suggests that the education of women may be the most effective means to reduce fertility, and fewer dependants may be a knock-on effect.[22]

Region of Residence

The variable *urban* was generally not significant either as a determinant of objective poverty or of household perception of their well-being, and this is consistent with the results from the ordinary least squares models in chapter 5. The result for 1997 was marginally significant and suggested that households residing in urban areas were 9.7 per cent less likely, compared to their rural counterparts, to classify themselves as poor. Controlling for the objectively poor, however, caused this effect to disappear. Differences in regional effects are more evident for households who fostered children.

The fostering of children, particularly when coupled with the region of residence, seems to have different effects on the likelihood of being poor. While the data suggest that households who fostered children are generally likely to be objectively poor, at no point was this result significant.

The interaction of this variable with area of residence in 1993 suggests that *urban households who fostered children* were, in fact, 8.8 per cent less likely to be objectively poor relative to their rural counterparts, while for the subjective poor, the variable was only marginally significant but suggested reduced likelihood that these households classify themselves as poor. The 1997 data, however, suggests a 9 per cent increase in the likelihood that households who fostered children classify themselves as poor. Similarly, having controlled for the objectively poor, there is an 8.2 per cent increase in the likelihood of households classifying themselves as poor. A reversal of this influence is seen in the 1999 data for urban households who have fostered-in children compared with the results in 1993 (cited above) for the objective poor. Here, urban households who fostered children were 12 per cent more likely to classify themselves as poor in comparison with rural households, with a 6 percentage points increase after controlling for the influence of the objectively poor. The results for the other years were not significant but suggested a reversal in the sign of the coefficient. These results suggest some level of instability in the perceived well-being of these households, possibly linked to the amount and frequency with which financial support for the children is received. These findings also support the theory of the importance of location-specific effects in influencing household perception of their well-being status. The results for 1993 may be due to households residing in urban areas perceiving their well-being to be higher than it actually is. It is quite likely that this perception is influenced by the relative level of social provisioning. It is well established in the literature that urban infrastructure tends to be more developed and of a better quality, and this is clearly the case in Jamaica. As such, household perception of its well-being may be influenced not just by private consumption, but also by its immediate social and physical environment.[23] The flip side to this argument may also be relevant to the 1999 data, since households in urban regions are also more likely to be exposed to a higher level of inequality and may require more resources to attain the socially accepted minimum well-being level. The results for 1999 may be influenced by the fact that these households perceived themselves to be poorer than they actually are estimated to be by the absolute poverty line methods and are more likely, relative to their rural counterparts, to classify themselves as poor.

Discussion and Conclusion

This section outlined the main findings and how far they are consistent with reality and the Jamaican literature. First, the educational attainment and gender of the household head was considered. These are important factors informing the perception of household well-being. Male-headed households have classified themselves as poor because they are relatively less well off, and the same is true for some single-female-headed households. There also appears to be some single-female-headed households who have higher educational outcomes but because of labour market distortions and hindrances to their socio-economic mobility, have classified themselves as poor. The actual well-being of these households is likely to be below their expected well-being and possibly one of the reasons for classifying themselves as poor.

Although the average level of consumption of poor male-headed households is no different from that of female-headed households, male-headed households are less likely to be objectively poor. The reason for this cannot be justified based on educational attainment, given women's higher educational attainment, but instead may be related to higher labour market participation rates of males, labour market distortions that favour males and the fact that males seem to gravitate to activities with greater risks, such as employment in the private sector, self-employment or in own-account activities.[24] In addition, mean salaries are higher in industries where men predominate. In fact, the results of 1999 surveys from large establishments (firms with at least ten persons) – excluding agriculture, public sector, private educational institutions and the free zones – showed that the mean income of all occupations within industry was greatest in electricity, gas and water, mining and transport, and storage and communication (PIOJ 2001). These industries have a greater proportion of male employees. This is also supported by Bailey (2003), who claims that the status accorded a profession is linked to the male to female ratio, with lower status, reflected in levels of salaries, being accorded to professions dominated by women; a case in point is teachers and nurses. Nevertheless, it may be that what seems to be discrimination against women is, in fact, the exercise of a choice where women prefer work in the public sector, possibly due to the higher levels of job security and flexible working hours.

Even in the light of the scenario above, single-female-headed house-holds, on average, consume more than the average of all other (subjectively poor) households, yet they are more likely to incorrectly classify themselves as poor. Part of the explanation lies in the discrimination they experi-ence in the labour market and the fact that their experience and educa-tional investment may not be commensurately rewarded relative to men. This has implications for the earnings premium associated with different levels of education and how the provision of education, and at what level, contributes to poverty reduction (Psacharopoulos and Chu Ng 1992). It is also possible that women may choose jobs that offer greater security at the expense of lower wages (Schultz 1989, 30), especially if there is no other stable source of income on which they may rely. Faced with these choices and labour market experience, single-female-headed households may per-ceive their well-being to be lower than that of similar households headed by males and may thus classify themselves as poor.

It is also likely that some single-female-headed households engaged in several livelihood strategies may gain substantial satisfaction from their independence and the creativity involved in the process, in addition to the higher income and level of consumption they tend to generate from such activities. This argument is clearly at odds with Adam Smith's (1910, 56–78) notion of work as toil and trouble or disutility in the sense suggested by John Stuart Mills (cited by Schumpeter 1994, 634–39) and may not reflect what is considered to be the norm. These households may still perceive their well-being to be lower than it actually is in the absence of a partner and may generally feel they struggle in order to survive.

The direction of influence of the child and old age dependency ratios for objectively poor households are the opposite for households classified as poor. This suggests that while poor households may be investing in the future of their children, coupled with continued contributions from elderly household members, households classified as poor are mortgaging the future of their children through their involvement in child labour and support of elderly dependants. A number of initiatives can be suggested: cash transfers, making schooling more attractive, legislation against the practice of child labour, minimum wage legislation, education of parents and support for the elderly. All of these may be pursued to solve the problem of child labour. These measures can benefit both poor and vulnerable households, but the appropriate response for poor households is a reduction in the number of child dependants.

In chapter 5, *household size* was not an important factor influencing the level of consumption of poor households, but it has a positive and significant influence on the probability of being poor. Similarly, household size also influenced household sense of well-being, possibly through its impact on living conditions. In addition, the area or region of residence influenced household perception of their well-being. The results suggest that while poor households who resided in urban areas may be worst off, they are likely to perceive their well-being as higher than it actually is and the converse may be true for non-poor households residing in rural areas. The level of development of the social and physical infrastructure and its quality may influence perception of well-being, but it is also quite likely that urban dwellers faced with higher levels of inequality may perceive their well-being as lower than suggested by the objective poverty line. In this light, household perception of their well-being may also be explained by their vulnerability to shocks and/or expectations and the relative weight assigned to these conditions versus current level of consumption.

The determinants of poverty generally point us to the causes and the possible remedial actions that may be taken to address the problem of poverty. Some of the indicators that determine poverty also influence household sense of well-being, albeit for different reasons. It is possible to address all of the factors that may cause poverty or cause households to classify themselves as poor, but it is still likely that some households may still perceive themselves as poor. This has implications for the indicators and strategies used in targeting households. For instance, female-headed households may be a legitimate group for targeted programmes directed at reducing poverty but, at the same time, some single-female-headed households may have incorrectly classified themselves as poor. They may therefore seek to register and participate in targeted programmes. To the extent that these households are vulnerable, their participation may be justifiable, but budgetary constraints may dictate that they are excluded. Understanding the reasons some households may incorrectly classify themselves as poor may offer insights that lead to improved targeting. The next chapter addresses the reasons households may incorrectly classify themselves as poor.

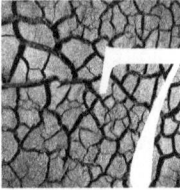

Why People Think They Are Poor
When They Are Not

This chapter analyses why people think they are poor when, objectively speaking, they are not. The results of this work suggest that households' understanding of their well-being is informed by their perceptions of their vulnerability to shocks and expectations, which are formed by the experiences and circumstances to which they are exposed. In this regard, single-female-headed households are particularly likely to incorrectly classify themselves as poor, due to, among other factors, their multiple sources of income, some of which are likely to be intermittent and unstable. These households may feel they are struggling in order to survive.

First, the approach used to model the reasons why households incorrectly classify themselves as poor is outlined. This is followed by an analysis of the results of probit and multinomial models. The reasons single-female-headed households are more likely to incorrectly classify themselves as poor is then further unpacked. In the last section, the conclusion paints the general picture and points to the implications of the findings.

Methodology

This section suggests approaches to analysing the reasons households may incorrectly classify themselves as poor. Two sets of probit models are estimated each year for poor households defined by both subjective and objective methods. The first set of models assigns 1 to those households who are unanimously poor (correctly classified as poor) and 0 to households incorrectly classified as poor.

$$y = \begin{cases} 1 & \textit{if } y^* > 0 \textit{ (unanimously poor)} \\ 0 & \textit{"incorrectly" poor} \end{cases} \tag{7.1}$$

Similarly, the second set of models assigns 1 to households correctly classified as poor and 0 to households incorrectly classified as not poor.

$$y = \begin{cases} 1 & \textit{if } y^* > 0 \textit{ (unanimously poor)} \\ 0 & \textit{"incorrectly" non-poor} \end{cases} \tag{7.2}$$

Table 7.1 identifies the groups of households described as correctly and incorrectly classified as poor. Households that are both objectively and subjectively poor are referred to as correctly classified or unanimously poor. On the other hand, objectively poor households who classify themselves as not poor are referred to as incorrectly not poor, while non-poor households self-classified as poor are seen as incorrectly poor.

The interest is in households who are classified as poor, but the likelihood of sample selection bias, though not evident or important, is also addressed. In general, sample selection bias refers to problems where the dependent variable is observed only for a restricted, non-random sample. This is typically seen in wage equations where one believes that union status has not only an intercept effect but also a slope effect (that is, the betas differ according to union status as well). This may be addressed by the

Table 7.1   Number of Cases of Households by Poverty Classification

Objective		Subjective	
		Poor (unanimously)	Non-poor ("incorrectly" non-poor)
Poor	1999	668	155
	1997	1,246	106
	1993	478	72
Non-poor ("incorrectly" poor)	1999	151	
	1997	105	
	1993	72	

Heckman's selection correction model (using a two-step estimation process where in the first stage a probit model is used to predict the probability of union status, and in the second stage, the inverse Mills's ratio is included as a regressor). In this chapter, the interest is in all the households who have classified themselves as poor and analysing the reasons some households are likely to incorrectly classify themselves as poor or non-poor. These households may be seen as a sample of interest or the set/population of subjective and objective poor, and sample selection is therefore not an issue. However, some may argue otherwise, and the robustness of the results is thus established through triangulation by estimating models that include all households and comparing the results with those previously generated. The multinomial models, including all households whose coefficients are expected to be consistent, give estimates which are then compared with the results of models based on all subjectively poor households. The results of the multinomial models for the pooled data are generally consistent with the results reported for the probit models.[1] The same variables are retained in all models for comparability and the signs of the significant coefficients point us to the reasons some households may incorrectly classify themselves as poor. In the next section, the results of the probit models (see appendix 4a–b, appendix 5a–b, and appendix 6a–b) are analysed.

Human Capital

Gender of Household Head

Chapters 5 and 6 demonstrated that the gender of the head of the household influences the well-being of households, and this remains the case in explaining the likelihood that households incorrectly classify themselves as poor. For both the subjective and objective poor, the variable *gender of household head* is only significant in 1999 and robust to alternative assumptions of economies of scale. However, the signs of the coefficients for the subjective and objective poor are the opposite. The data suggest that male-headed households are 62.1 per cent less likely to incorrectly classify themselves as poor than subjectively poor female-headed households, and 6.1 per cent more likely to correctly classify themselves as poor relative to objectively poor female-headed households. The latter result is possibly due to the relatively large number of poor single-female-headed households and their tendency to incorrectly classify themselves as not poor. The result for the subjective poor may reflect the strong correlation (–0.81), between the variables *male-headed households* and *single-female-headed households*, pointing to a large number of female-headed households who are single. As a result, the variable *gender* was dropped from the model estimated for the subjective poor. This means that the results for the objective poor in 1999, if viewed in isolation from other results, run counter to the general literature on female headship.

The results for the subjective poor show that single-female-headed households are, on average, 9.2 per cent less likely to correctly classify themselves as poor relative to male-headed households and female-headed households who are married or in a common law relationship. At the same time, objectively poor single-female-headed households are, on average, 9.7 per cent more likely to correctly classify themselves as poor relative to the comparison categories. These results suggest that there are single-female-headed households who are not poor but who incorrectly classify themselves as poor, while there are objectively poor male-headed households, female-headed households and single-female-headed households who may not classify themselves as poor and, among these households, single-female-headed households may be significantly poorer. The results also suggest that both female and male single household heads as a group were more likely to incorrectly classify themselves as poor, supporting the literature suggesting that single individuals are likely to report lower levels of well-being than married individuals. However, while single-female-headed households consume approximately 29.1 per cent less than single-male-headed households, the difference between households incorrectly classified as poor is only 3.0 per cent. Single-female-headed households also have an average of four members, twice the household size of single-male-headed households, supporting the general tendency for female-headed households to have a larger number of children. The influence of the number of children on household perception of their well-being is assessed, as in previous chapters, using the child dependency ratio.

Child Dependency Ratio

The literature on child dependants, for example Lipton and Ravallion (1995), recognizes the subjective utility of child-bearing, but generally sees an additional child as a net user of household resources. Children perform simple unpaid household chores, which otherwise may have to be paid for. If these income-saving tasks are similar and general across all households, no difference in the effect of the child dependency ratio is expected. It is also known that children from poor households tend to be employed in these tasks to a greater extent. In keeping with the results of the ordinary least squares models, the sign of the coefficient for the objectively poor is consistent with expectations; however, for the subjective poor there are counter-intuitive results. The results above suggest that subjectively poor households incorrectly classify themselves as poor since their consumption levels are attained because their children are involved in economic activities, which may also be undertaken at the expense of their educations.[2] There are two possible factors motivating these households to incorrectly classify themselves as poor. First, they are likely to be relatively poorer compared to other households, especially in the absence of support from their children. Second, the economic activities in which their children are engaged are likely to be unstable and uncertain so that earnings may vary from week to week. Coupled with the sacrifice of their children's education, their uncertainty about future well-being may also lead them to perceive their household as poor.[3] This is particularly the case if these household heads were themselves involved in child labour and see little or no prospects of breaking the intergenerational cycle.

Elderly Dependency Ratio

The *elderly dependency ratio* is significant in 1999 and 1993 (marginally) but only for subjectively poor households, and it is generally consistent with the findings in chapters 5 and 6. Each additional elderly household member per working-age adult increases the probability of being correctly classified as poor by an average of 16.1 per cent. This suggests that households with a larger number of elderly dependants – especially if this number has increased as shown in the national estimates – coupled with low or no pensions may experience a downward movement in their consumption. They will possibly have lower expectations of improved well-being, hence the tendency to classify themselves as poor, and indeed, they are more likely to be so. Similarly, household heads with a disability are more likely to be correctly classified as poor. Of the objective and subjective poor, these households are, respectively, 6.8 per cent and 5.8 per cent more likely to be poor.

Household Size

Once adjustments are made for economies of scale, *household size* and the square of this variable are not determinants of objective poverty. In the absence of adjustment for economies of scale, the coefficient of both variables is significant and suggests that each additional household member increases the probability that households correctly classified themselves as poor by 0.3 per cent, but at a declining rate, with turning point at thirteen household members. A somewhat different picture emerges for the subjectively poor households, suggesting that *household size* and the square of the variable are generally significant determinants of being correctly classified as poor. On average, an additional household member increases the likelihood of being correctly classified as poor by 6.3 per cent, with turning points varying between six and ten members.

Education of Principal Earner

None of the educational variables for the principal earner significantly influences whether an objectively poor household classifies itself as poor or not. The results for the subjective poor indicate, however, that the coefficients are marginally significant in the 1999 and 1993 data. They point to inconsistency in the signs of the coefficients for those with *secondary* education. The 1999 data suggest that principal earners with basic (7.2 per cent) or secondary (13.1 per cent) education were less likely to correctly classify themselves as poor, relative to those with tertiary education, and are at odds with the findings for 1993, which suggest that heads with secondary education were 3.3 per cent more likely to correctly classify themselves as poor.

Social Capital

The variables that are important in household perception of their well-being are *support from friends and family, health insurance* coverage and the *fostering-in* of children. The receipt of support from friends and relatives living in Jamaica is associated with increased probability of being correctly classified as poor and is true for both rural and urban dwellers receiving this type of assistance. While subjectively poor households with health insurance coverage are more likely to incorrectly classify themselves as poor, the opposite is true for the objectively poor. In addition, objectively poor households residing in urban regions and with health insurance coverage are more likely to incorrectly classify themselves as not poor. This result may be informed by the fact that these individuals are employed and have a stable source of income.

Households caring for children whose parents live elsewhere are likely to be correctly classified as poor. This variable is marginally significant at the lower limit of economies of scale for both the subjective and objective poor. At the higher limit of economies of scale and in the absence of any adjustment for economies of scale, the coefficient for the subjective poor is significant. On average, these households are 3.5 per cent more likely to correctly classify themselves as poor compared with the rest of subjectively poor households not receiving this form of assistance in 1993. The corresponding coefficient for objectively poor households in 1997 is 0.3 per cent.

Financial Capital

Generally, the sector of employment is unimportant except in the case of the subjective poor for 1999. Principal earners employed in the *agricultural sector* are 8 per cent more likely to be correctly classified as poor, and this is robust for all assumptions of economies of scales. In addition, an increase in the *ratio of unemployed adults to those employed* increases the probability of being correctly classified as poor, varying between 11.6 per cent for the objective poor in 1999 and 3.6 per cent for the subjective poor in 1997.

Physical Capital

Both housing quality and ownership of durable assets are important considerations for households in classifying their well-being. Households who did not use electricity as their main source of lighting, had no piped water into their dwelling or premises and shared a kitchen were more likely to correctly classify themselves as poor. However, an additional room increases the probability of objectively poor households incorrectly classifying themselves as not poor. These households occupy, on average, four rooms, compared with two rooms for those correctly classified as poor.[4] For the subjective poor, the variable *room* is only marginally significant when economies of scale equal zero, and only in 1999 is the square of room significant. This suggests that the relationship between the number of rooms and household perception of their well-being is not linear, suggesting that there are economies to be had in the sharing of living space. Beyond a certain number of rooms, households will not be correctly classified as poor. The turning point for this relationship occurs at four rooms, both when adjustments are and are not made for economies of scale.

The results of the probit, multinomial and ordinary least squares models are generally consistent, and where there are differences, important insights into the reasons are gleaned. Why do some poor single-female-headed households incorrectly identify themselves as not poor, while some non-poor single-female-headed households incorrectly classify themselves as poor, and how these results differ for the rest of households? This is the concern of the next section.

The Paradox of Wealth and Vulnerability

The likelihood of single-female-headed households incorrectly classified as poor or not poor is unpacked further by considering their educational attainment, area of residence, employment status, income support and the contribution of income support to their consumption. The section begins by looking at the educational attainment of single-female-headed households.

Educational Attainment

The distribution of household heads by the level of educational attainment, proxied by the last school attended, shows that most heads have only primary education or less (68.3 per cent), and in cases where they are classified as having secondary education (27.6 per cent), this really refers to the completion of the seventh to ninth grade at an All Age School or Primary Junior High School. Although the curriculum is different from the primary level, the level of work done is generally below that of secondary schools, and the aggregation is thus most convenient in terms of years of schooling.

Turning to the academic achievement of household heads, proxied by the highest examination passed in the 1999 data, the results show that

Table 7.2   Last School Attended, 1999, 1997 and 1993

School Type	"Incorrectly" Poor		"Incorrectly" Not Poor		Unanimously Poor		Not Poor	
	SFHH	Other	SFHH	Other	SFHH	Other	SFHH	Other
Basic	1.6	0.0	16.7	2.8	0.0	0.0	0.0	0.0
Primary	35.2	44.5	55.7	61.4	57.7	54.5	33.6	41.5
Secondary	57.4	50.5	22.0	33.1	36.2	40.4	42.3	46.7
Tertiary	7.0	3.5	0.0	4.2	3.3	2.5	22.1	14.0
None	0.0	1.4	0.0	0.6	2.6	2.3	0.1	0.3

Source: PIOJ various years.

their academic achievement is very low. Most of these household heads (79.7 per cent) have not passed any examinations, and it is likely that all of these individuals would have had only a primary education. At the end of the sixth year, they would have attended a primary all age school – having failed the Common Entrance Examination, an additional three years is spent, at the end of which the Grade Nine Achievement Tests are taken. Those who pass this examination and find a place in a secondary school may go on to take the GCE or CXC examination, otherwise they have to leave school at this point, and previously, no certificate of achievement was given. On average, most of these individuals have nine years of schooling, which is equivalent to the third year of secondary schooling, but this comparison is not legitimate since the curriculum is invariably different.

The disaggregation of educational attainment by household self-classification of their well-being suggests similar results. Most of the heads of households correctly classified as poor had either primary (56.1 per cent) or secondary (38.3 per cent) education. This group of households also account for the largest proportion of heads with no formal education. Here again, a larger proportion of single-female-headed households are in this group. The distributions of the educational attainment of heads of households incorrectly classified as poor and not poor show a similar clustering around primary and secondary educational attainment. However, these groups also had a noticeable proportion of heads with tertiary education, varying between 5.3 per cent and 2.1 per cent respectively. In fact, households incorrectly classified as poor had the highest proportion of heads with secondary education (53.9 per cent), and among this group, the proportion of single-female-headed households with secondary and tertiary education was even higher at 57.4 per cent and 7.0 per cent respectively. The situation is no different after disaggregating by the gender of the household head. There is no difference in the average years of schooling of male-headed households and female-headed households, and their scholastic achievements, both in terms of years of schooling and highest examination passed, are low. However, a slightly higher proportion of single-female-headed households achieved slightly better educational outcomes than the rest of household heads.[5]

Why are some single-female-headed households incorrectly classifying themselves as poor while others who are indeed poor are not? Part of the reasons for these results may be related to relative adaptive expectations of attainable well-being, where expected well-being is a generally increasing function of educational attainment. The extent of the divergence between actual well-being and expected well-being may also influence the perception of the households of their poverty status. When aspirations are frustrated, people perceive themselves as poor. Poor households who have incorrectly classified themselves as not poor have lower levels of educational attainment (shown in table 7.2 by the higher level of clustering in the categories Basic and Primary) and lower-than-average levels of expected well-being, but their responses may also be influenced by pride and stigma.

Area of Residence

The area of residence also influences household perception of well-being. Households in poor areas may perceive themselves as poor even when they are not. Of those households correctly classified as poor, 62.2 per cent resided in rural areas, while for households incorrectly classified as poor or not poor, 50.0 per cent of each group resided in rural areas. Further, disaggregation by the gender of head reveals that most of the single-female-headed households who are poor but incorrectly classified as not poor resided in the KMA (29.4 per cent) or other towns (28.5 per cent). For single-female-headed households incorrectly classified as poor, the difference in the proportion residing in urban and rural areas is not significant.[6]

Employment Status

The industry of employment of the principal earner is generally not significant, but an interesting contrast emerges on considering the sector of employment of the principal earner (see table 7.3). Most of the heads of objectively poor households are employed in own-account activities (normally seen as largely informal activities), and these account for the lowest proportion employed in central or local government agencies. Households incorrectly classified as poor had an equal proportion of principal earners in own-account activities and the private sector, together accounting for 85 per cent, while households incorrectly classified as not

Table 7.3   Employment Status of Principal Earner

Sector of Employment	"Incorrectly" Poor		"Incorrectly" Not Poor		Unanimously Poor		Not Poor	
	SFHH	Other	SFHH	Other	SFHH	Other	SFHH	Other
1999								
Local or central government	11.7	5.5	–	8.7	6.1	1.8	20.4	11.3
Other government agencies	3.3	–	–	1.6	1.1	1.8	3.6	2.4
Private sector	48.5	38.2	33.3	28.6	44.2	32.0	50.3	43.1
Unpaid family worker	–	–	–	–	–	0.6	–	–
Employer	–	1.8	–	0.8	0.6	–	1.2	2.1
Own-account worker	36.7	54.6	66.7	60.0	48.1	63.6	24.0	40.8
1997								
Local or central government	10.2	6.3	37.5	7.7	7.0	4.6	16.4	12.6
Other government agencies	10.4	–	–	5.1	2.1	2.2	7.8	4.3
Private sector	39.6	58.3	25.0	28.2	54.4	41.6	56.0	44.8
Unpaid family worker	–	–	–	1.3	–	–	–	0.2
Employer	–	–	–	–	–	0.7	3.5	2.1
Own-account worker	39.6	35.4	37.5	57.7	36.2	50.9	16.4	35.8
1993								
Local or central government	25.0	7.1	–	2.0	7.0	2.4	16.5	10.2
Other government agencies	0.0	8.9	–	–	2.3	2.4	2.7	2.9
Private sector	41.7	26.8	40.0	29.4	32.6	32.9	51.1	43.5
Unpaid family worker	–	–	–	–	–	0.3	–	0.1
Employer	–	–	–	–	–	–	0.5	0.9
Own-account worker	33.3	57.1	60.0	58.1	58.1	61.6	28.7	42.2

Source: PIOJ various years.

poor were employed primarily in the private sector or own-account activities, with the latter sector accounting for approximately two-thirds of these households. Non-poor households, on the other hand, are predominantly employed in the private sector (48.1 per cent), and this group also has the largest proportion of households in government agencies and, not surprisingly, the lowest proportion in own-account activities. In general, a greater proportion of single-female-headed households are employed either by government agencies or by the private sector. These differences are greatest in the government sector among households incorrectly classified as poor and in the private sector for those poor households incorrectly classified as not poor. How far is household self-classification linked to the perception that wages are higher in the private sector and lower in government agencies?

Income Support

Child Fostering

Of all households receiving support for children they have fostered in, the majority (66.9 per cent) are headed by females, of which 80.1 per cent are single-female-headed households. Of the single-female-headed households who are unanimously poor, an average of 37.4 per cent received this form of assistance, compared with 49.1 per cent of those who have incorrectly classified themselves as poor. As a group, subjectively poor single-female-headed households generally have the highest proportionate rate of receipt of child support. This is not surprising, since based on the 1999 data, 32.9 per cent of the children of the head or spouse receive child support from a parent who lives elsewhere, compared with 57.9 per cent of those who live in single-female-headed households.[7] It may also be that these households are more willing to take on fostering responsibilities since the additional child does not proportionately increase child care responsibilities and serves as a valuable source of income. The greater likelihood of child fostering in these households may also be related to the degree of influence or autonomy exercised by women in the decision-making process, as suggested by Castle (1995, 689), in reference to Mali.

Remittances

There is no official estimate of the amount of money in the form of remittances that enters Jamaica annually, but from the data, it is substantial. Remittances go not only to the household head but also to several individuals – lump sums may be received to be shared among several household members. Nonetheless, when the other members of the household are siblings, it can be anticipated that the head of the household will exercise some control over how the monies are spent, consistent with the focus of the analysis on the household head. The receipt of remittance from relatives and friends "a foreign" by headship shows that an average of 48.3 per cent of households receiving this form of assistance are female-headed households, while an average of 54.2 per cent of households assisted by friends and family who live in Jamaica are female-headed households, of whom approximately 80.0 per cent are single-female-headed households. The proportion of single-female-headed households receiving assistance from individuals residing abroad is also higher: 68 per cent. In fact, table 7.4 shows that a higher proportion of single-female-headed households who

Table 7.4   Average Rate of Assistance or Participation in Social Programmes

	"Incorrectly" Poor		"Incorrectly" Not Poor		Unanimously Poor		Not Poor	
	SFHH	Other	SFHH	Other	SFHH	Other	SFHH	Other
Support for children whose parents live elsewhere	49.1	20.2	4.2	14.2	37.4	19.8	22.0	11.9
Support from friends and family in Jamaica	30.8	14.6	37.8	21.5	40.5	26.4	24.7	14.1
Remittance	45.3	31.7	47.7	38.7	37.4	26.8	38.9	32.6
Social security (NIS)	3.7	3.6	11.1	7.8	9.9	7.0	8.2	6.6
Private govt or other pension fund	1.2	0.7	9.7	3.9	4.3	2.5	3.5	2.3
"Public assistance, poor relief & food stamps"	9.9	4.6	5.6	11.0	28.2	20.7	3.4	4.4

Source: PIOJ 1999, 1997, 1993.

are objectively poor (averaging 40.5 per cent) receive support from relatives and friends residing in Jamaica followed by those poor single-female-headed households who have incorrectly classified themselves as not poor. While the proportion of single-female-headed households receiving remittances is, generally, highest among poor households incorrectly classified as not poor, it is not much greater compared with non-poor households incorrectly classified as poor. Some idea of the actual contribution of remittance to household's consumption expenditure is therefore essential and is illustrated next.

Social and Safety Net Programmes

Single-female-headed households have a slightly higher average proportionate rate of participation in social protection programmes such as health insurance, pensions and the National Insurance Scheme. In the case of the safety net programmes – public assistance, poor relief and food stamps – the participation rate of single-female-headed households is significantly higher for households objectively poor and incorrectly classified as poor, while among poor households incorrectly classified as not poor, single-female-headed households had a proportionately lower rate of participation (see table 7.4). In fact, the data for 1997 and 1993 show that these households did not receive any pensions and did not participate in the safety net programmes. The participation in social protection programmes clearly refers to the current and previous levels of labour market participation of men and women, but single-female-headed households make a greater effort and are participating to a larger extent in safety net programmes than other households, in particular those single-female-headed households incorrectly classified as poor. Is this out of need or greed? These results imply that these households may not rely solely on women's labour market activities for their financial support. Therefore, any analysis of their time use must consider their participation in social safety net programmes, especially where long waiting time to collect the benefit is evident.

Based on their human capital endowment, single-female-headed households are at a comparable level with male-headed households, yet their levels of consumption, in some cases, surpass those of male-headed households. The explanation clearly lies in the higher rate of participation by single-female-headed households in social programmes and their receipt of remittances and other forms of support. This also suggests that although single-female-headed households may be faring better than male-headed households, they are clearly much more vulnerable to economic shocks, both in the local and in the foreign economy. Of interest also is the extent to which single-female-headed households have to forego leisure in order to achieve their current levels of well-being.[8] Naturally, some idea of their time use may be informative. Handa (1998) examined the time use of male-headed households and female-headed households (71.3 per cent are single-female-headed households) using the JSLC and Labour Force (1993) data sets and found that the mean total hours worked by female-headed household was 48.9 compared to 47.3 for male-headed household. While women spent an equal amount of time at home and in paid employment, men primarily spend their time in paid employment. When leisure is accounted for, Handa (1998) found that the proportion of female-headed households and male-headed households that were poor changed marginally (less than 1 percentage point) and the "relative disparity in welfare between female-headed households and male-headed households remained essentially unchanged". Although this finding is revealing, it does not account for variations within groups. Using the combined data sets, it is possible to examine the time spent by single-female-headed households on their main job for a reference week. Not surprisingly, they spent, on average, approximately forty hours, the same as that of other household heads.

Contribution of Assistance to Household Consumption

Further light may be shed on the relative rates of assistance or participation in social programmes by establishing the average amounts received and their contribution to total household consumption. The analysis focuses on the monies received from family and friends. Unlike the 1993 data, where there are no missing values for amounts received as remittances, child support and support from friends and family living in Jamaica, the 1999 and 1997 data sets have a significant number of cases where the household identifies itself as receiving these forms of support but does not state the amount. If estimates are made using the average monies based on those households reporting receipt and the amounts received, there will be a selection problem. Using the Heckman selection equation, it is possible to predict the amount received and establish the extent to which these support mechanisms contribute to household well-being and possibly inform perception of poverty status. The variables used in predicting remittances and child support are as follows: relationship of the child or individual receiving the benefit to the head of the household who is assumed to be the principal caregiver (grandchild, child of spouse, relative and not relative, the excluded or comparison category is the head or parent of the child); male child; female child; three dummy variables for grade of child; basic and primary (child attending secondary school is the excluded category); union status; urban; partner; and log total consumption expenditure. The elderly dependency ratio was included in predicting support from friends and relatives living in Jamaica. The Heckman model was used where the first part is a probit equation for whether the household receives remittances or not. The Heckman selection equation assumes the underlying regression relationship:

$$y_j = x_j\beta + \varepsilon_{1j} \tag{7.3}$$

where y_j are monies received from parents for children living within the household and from friends or relatives living in Jamaica or abroad. The dependent variable is, however, not always observed even when households indicated that they received these forms of support.[9] In the 1997 data there

Table 7.5 Mean Income Support from Friends and Relatives

	1999		1997		1993	
	J$	US$ avg.	J$	US$ avg.	J$	US$ avg.
Remittance	10,673.33	272.28	10,093.83	284.33	2,662.10	106.83
Predicted remittance	17,332.77	442.16	17,280.97	486.79		
Family support	3,937.52	100.45	3,279.74	92.39	843.77	33.86
Predicted support	4,347.98	110.92	3,226.35	90.88		
Child support	8,478.82	216.30	8,098.41	228.12	1,563.10	62.72
Predicted child support	8,527.86	217.55	11,172.38	314.71		

Note: The annual average exchange rates of the Jamaican dollar to the US dollar are 39.2, 35.5 and 24.92 for the periods 1999, 1997 and 1993 respectively.

Source: PIOJ 1993–99.

were forty-two, forty-five and seventy such cases, while in the 1999 data an average of twenty-five cases were missing.[10] The dependent variable for observation j is observed if

$$z_j \gamma + \varepsilon_{2j} > 0 \qquad\qquad (7.4)$$

where

$$\varepsilon_1 \sim N(0, \sigma)$$
$$\varepsilon_2 \sim N(0, 1)$$
$$corr(\varepsilon_1, \varepsilon_2) = \rho \neq 0$$

Heckman produces consistent, asymptotically efficient estimates for all parameters, and the results of the predictions, if greater than zero, replace the missing values in the estimates. The estimates in table 7.5 report the means prior to and after adjustments for predicted values. These show that with the exception of remittances, the estimates are comparable. It is suspected that some elements of remittance are included in both family and child support, but the extent of this cannot be established.

The 1999 and 1997 data in table 7.6 show that the share of remittance in household consumption is greatest for poor single-female-headed households incorrectly classified as not poor.[11] However, these households had the lowest share of remittance in 1993. In addition, in keeping with their lower rates of participation in social programmes, the share of monies received from these programmes was, generally, lowest.

For the period under review, single-female-headed households incorrectly classified as poor and those unanimously poor depended to a larger extent on other forms of support to cushion their consumption, with these monies being of greater importance for the latter group. This finding points to an unsubstantiated notion that women may use pregnancy and children as means of securing financial support from males and, possibly, other family members.

Conclusion

The aim of this conclusion is not to repeat the plethora of empirical issues and findings put forward, but rather to paint the general picture that emerges. It is clear from the findings that the factors associated with people's

Table 7.6 Remittance and Other Assistance and Shares in Total Consumption

	Incorrectly Poor		Incorrectly Not Poor		Unanimously Poor		Not Poor	
	SFHH	Other	SFHH	Other	SFHH	Other	SFHH	Other
1999								
Predicted remittance	21,581.43	10,708.66	26,072.38	15,787.65	12,292.30	12,921.90	23,081.73	19,551.44
Remittance	15,001.19	3,335.47	11,600.00	10,343.80	8,289.13	7,307.57	14,457.16	12,184.96
Predicted child support	14,005.21	4,331.03	0	6,502.81	16,394.80	3,599.75	11,335.10	7,346.30
Child support	14,482.93	4,651.85	0	6,548.25	16,394.88	3,536.36	11,173.85	7,308.73
Predicted family support	4,709.41	1,800.57	3,250.00	3,323.49	6,358.24	6,192.10	4,262.64	3,013.31
Family support	4,741.18	481.13	3,250.00	2,782.27	5,981.15	5,835.81	4,059.28	2,570.42
Share of remittance in consumption	0.1	0.07	0.2	0.09	0.1	0.14	0.09	0.08
Share of total support in consumption	0.1	0.03	0.02	0.05	0.19	0.13	0.05	0.04
1997								
Predicted remittance	18,495.98	22,521.29	30,751.47	14,893.73	18,853.03	10,613.02	24,193.33	24,322.37
Remittance	14,957.32	3,947.50	6,328.57	7,607.86	10,266.71	6,424.67	12,139.17	15,491.60
Predicted child support	34,907.76	15,678.46	2,250.00	3,705.25	23,569.71	6,013.14	18,105.00	5,025.50
Child support	26,625.47	3,659.09	2,250.00	2,540.92	17,517.95	5,156.90	15,495.21	2,282.08
Predicted family support	9,464.90	1,187.50	3,187.50	3,062.22	4,584.44	2,204.84	8,119.22	1,945.96
Family support	9,765.46	1,212.77	3,187.50	3,131.82	4,717.80	2,239.25	8,233.90	1,980.24
Share of remittance in consumption	0.06	0.08	0.39	0.12	0.14	0.09	0.14	0.09
Share of total support in consumption	0.18	0.08	0.05	0.04	0.23	0.07	0.11	0.03
1993								
Remittance	2,920.00	2,955.44	244.00	1,425.08	1,626.67	1,657.98	3,740.77	2,822.10
Child support	6,420.00	2,584.21	0.00	695.16	1,156.00	1,400.25	1,742.97	1,493.02
Family support	760.00	1,347.18	450.00	472.58	1,522.00	738.64	1,229.14	727.34
Share of remittance in consumption	0.04	0.03	0.01	0.05	0.05	0.04	0.05	0.03
Share of total support in consumption	0.11	0.05	0.02	0.07	0.14	0.09	0.09	0.06

Source: PIOJ various years.

perception of their poverty status is dynamic, and not only based on their current levels of consumption but also related to the perception of their vulnerability and expectations of current and future well-being. The differences in these factors, highlighted over the period of this study, also point to the importance of historical measurement errors that may arise in using cross-sectional data for one period. Seeking to control for possible historical measurement errors by the use of data for three years, spread over the 1990s, mean income regressions, probit and multinomial models were used. These models have revealed that the characteristics of the poor are not static and neither are the reasons for incorrectly classifying a household as poor or not poor. These results may also be influenced by the movement of households in and out of poverty over the period. It is also recognized that there are other psychological and sociological factors that cannot be quantified but may motivate households to classify themselves as poor.

While male-headed households fared and continue to fare better than female-headed households in general, single-female-headed households do as well in terms of consumption as male-headed households, but they are more likely to incorrectly perceive themselves as poor. The comparable level of well-being for single-female-headed households seems to have been attained through a higher level of dependency on friends and family, child support, remittances and participation in social programmes, making them more vulnerable to economic and social shocks, and more likely to incorrectly classify themselves as poor. Clearly, this reveals one of the limitations of the objective consumption poverty approach, as it does not consider how household consumption levels have been attained or what sacrifices and costs are involved. But single-female-headed households' decision to incorrectly classify themselves as poor may also be influenced by the fact that if single-female-headed households total consumption is reduced by the various amount of support they receive, they are likely to fare worse than male-headed households, even though single-female-headed households have higher educational attainment. This coupled with higher expectations of attainable well-being makes it not surprising that they are incorrectly classifying themselves as poor.

At the same time, there are poor single-female-headed households incorrectly self-classified as not poor, possibly influenced by the relatively large proportion of their consumption that is accounted for by remittances. This may give households some sense of security against price rises that are influenced by the continuous depreciation of the Jamaican dollar. They are also dwelling in houses that are likely to be larger and have more rooms. Not only may this influence their perception of their well-being, but others within their community may also perceive them to be better off than they actually are, even though it is quite likely that their homes are owned by family or friends living abroad. In addition, unlike single-female-headed households incorrectly classified as poor, the average educational attainment of poor single-female-headed house-holds incorrectly classified as not poor is lower than average, and they have the lowest participation rate in public assistance, poor relief and the social welfare programme. The heads of these households are also likely to be employed, thus enjoying the benefits of health insurance, and also likely to reside in urban areas. It is quite likely that these households may therefore choose not to participate in programmes targeted at the poor since they do not see themselves as poor.

The direction of influence of the child dependency ratio for households correctly classified as poor is consistent with expectations; however, the opposite is the case for households incorrectly classified as poor. These households are likely to be less well off in the absence of income support from their children, who are also at risk of various forms of exploitations, and their earnings are likely to be unstable and uncertain. Coupled with the sacrifice of their education, it is not surprising that these households are incorrectly classifying themselves as poor. The decision to incorrectly classify themselves as poor may also be informed by their aspirations and low expectations for their children's future well-being. This is consistent with the literature which argues that poor households, even if trapped in poverty, aspire to get their children out of it, even if they see no possibility of getting out themselves.

It was established in chapter 5 that household size is not an important variable in explaining the level of consumption of objectively poor house-holds. The importance of household size is, however, seen for households incorrectly classified as poor. The results also suggest that the composition of the household and whether the household head has a disability or not are important. Households whose head has a disability are likely to be correctly classified as poor. In addition, unlike those households correctly classified as poor, the elderly in households incorrectly classified as not poor are net contributors to these households' resources. On the other hand, the greater level of dependency of the elderly in some households, possibly compounded by the lack of the likelihood of a significant inheritance, results in households having low expectations of improved well-being and are correctly classifying themselves as poor.

The results consistently suggest that households in receipt of assistance for child care and monies from friends and family living in Jamaica are more likely to be poor. This is consistent with the feeling of responsibility to help less fortunate relatives and friends that was expressed in community focus group meetings of those who have escaped poverty or are somewhat better off. The amounts received for child care are, however, much more than from friends and family and this is a clear responsibility. To the extent that family support is also seen as a responsibility and a continuous transfer to poor households, it clearly presents as drag on the well-being of households who may still be at the margins or just above the poverty threshold. While the analysis looked at the effect of monies received on household consumption and perception of well-being, research into obligations such as child care as well as the monies provided by friends and family and how this influences perception of well-being is also needed. This may also allow us to understand some of the motives for fostering out children.

A large proportion of principal earners in households correctly classified as poor are involved in own-account activities. Similarly, households whose principal earner is employed in the agricultural sector are also more likely to be correctly classified as poor. Subjectively poor households have a larger proportion of workers in government services, and a larger proportion of poor households self-classified as not poor work in the private sector. Though not very clear, it is possible that differential sectoral growth rates (inequality held constant) may also influence households' perception of their well-being status.

Finally, not only has the extent to which the objective methodology accords with the households' perception of their well-being been established, but the difference between household perception of their well-being and their objective poverty status reflects information that has not been explored but may prove useful for policy purposes. This suggests a different approach to establishing vulnerability based on the perceptions and experiences of households of their well-being levels relative to what is deemed the minimum necessary level of well-being at a given time. For instance, households whose consumption level is consistently just below the poverty line may not consider themselves as poor, and this may apply to all households whose consumption is above some critically expected level. On the other hand, it may be possible that households are not defined as poor by the objective method at some given point but, due to uncertainty relating to their source of income or other risk factors, the household may define itself as poor. As a result, the decision to classify the households as poor or not is informed by individual perception of vulnerability to shocks and individual expectations, which are formed by the experiences and circumstances to which different households are exposed. To the extent that household experience spells of poverty, they are also likely to classify themselves as poor even if they have moved above the poverty threshold at some given point. The subjective poverty approach presented in this book has provided an alternative view of the poverty situation and the fact that households' view of their well-being may not correspond with the objective approach. This information has implications for the design of poverty alleviation policies and the targeting indicators used, and it may allow for improved allocation of increasingly scarce resources to the poor.

APPENDIX

1

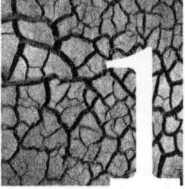

Description of Variables

	DEMOGRAPHICS		
Human capital	GENDER	Male (female – excluded category)	1,0
	CHILD_DEPEND	Children as proportion of working-age adults	continuous
	ELDERLY_DEPEND	Elderly as proportion of working-age adults	continuous
	HHSIZE	HH size	discrete
	HHSIZESQ	HH size squared	discrete
	AGE	Age of HH head	discrete
	AGESQ	Age square of HH head	discrete
	DISABLED	HH head has some form of disability	1,0
	UNION STATUS	Married husband/wife or common law	1,0
	SINGLE HEAD	HH headed by single female	1,0
	FEMALEHEAD	HH headed by female who is married or in common-law relationship	1,0
	PARTNER	Partner does not reside within household	1,0
	URBAN	Urban	1,0
	HEALTH AND WELFARE		
Social Capital	INSURANCE	Health insurance coverage	1,0
	REMITTANCE	Support from relatives and friends living abroad	1,0
	SUPPORT	From Jamaica relatives and friends living in Jamaica	1,0
	FOSTERED IN	Support for children whose parent or parents live else where	1,0
	EDUCATION OF HEAD		
Financial Capital	NOEDUC	No education	1,0
	BASICEDUC	Primary education	1,0
	SECEDUC	Secondary education	1,0
	PROP UNEMPLOYED	Proportion of adult HH members in labour force unemployed	continuous
	OCCUPATION OF HH HEAD		
	AGRICULTURAL WORKER	Farmers, loggers, fisherman and hunters	1,0
	SERVICE WORKER	Clerks, protective service workers, street vendors and helpers, labourers and sales persons	1,0
	HOUSING CONDITIONS		
Physical Capital	ROOMS	Number of rooms	discrete
	ROOMSQ	Number of rooms squared	discrete
	WATER	Stand pipe, well, spring, rain and other (indoor and outdoor tap excluded)	1,0
	TENURE	Owned land on which dwelling stands	1,0
	TELEPHONE	Dwelling has a telephone.	1,0
	LIGHTING	Main source of lighting – kerosene, other and none	1,0
	SHAREKITCHEN	Share kitchen (excluded category – exclusive use and none)	1,0
	OWNERSHIP OF ASSETS		
	SEWING-MACH	Sewing machine	1,0
	GSTOVE	Gas stove	1,0
	ESTOVE	Electric stove	1,0
	RFRIGE	Refrigerator	1,0
	RADIO	Radio	1,0
	STEREO	Stereo	1,0
	VIDEO	Video	1,0
	WASHMACH	Washing machine	1,0
	TV	Television	1,0
	VEHICLES	Motor vehicle	1,0

Source: PIOJ various years.

Minimum Survival Needs as a Function of Consumption

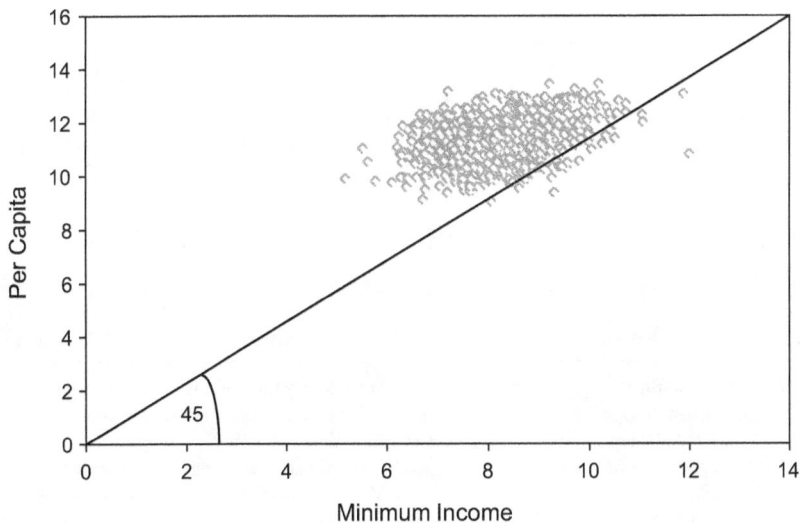

Source: PIOJ 1999.

Subjective Thresholds Set at the Maximum and Median, 1999

Area	Adult Equivalent Per Capita Consumption				Minimum Survival Requirements			
	Maximum	P_0	Median	P_0	Maximum	P_0	Median	P_0
KMA	109,036.4	55.6	54,283.0	17.5	250,018.0	88.9	13,649.8	0.66
Other Towns	101,298.7	65.3	46,143.0	20.0	21,471.1	0.29	9,438.4	0
Rural Areas	107,493.4	84.3	42,221.6	28.3	24,546.4	8.1	6,875.4	0.32
Jamaica	106,878.5	71.7	46,810.5	23.3	96,619.0	32.7	9,517.5	0.34

Note: Jamaica estimates are weighted. The maximum MSR for the KMA is an outlier and in fact when dropped the threshold is 35,167, with a corresponding headcount of 6.9 for the KMA. When this in taken into consideration the headcount for Jamaica is 6.3 per cent. On the other hand, the poverty gaps based on the thresholds at the maximum and median consumption of households classified as poor are 45.0 per cent and 28.6 per cent respectively and reflects the amount of resources needed on average to bring the poor up to the poverty line.

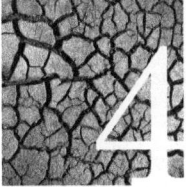

Probit Marginal and Impact Effects

Appendix 4a Probit Marginal and Impact Effects: The Probability of Being Unanimously Poor (Subjective Self-Classification, 1999)

	(1)	(2)	(3)		(1)	(2)	(3)
CHIDEPEND	-0.051	-0.034	-0.056	PERUEMP	0.066	0.087	0.069
	0.015**	0.015*	0.015**		0.048	0.046+	0.052
OLDDEPEND	0.239	0.256	0.167	SEWMACH	0.024	0.007	0.034
	0.059**	0.056**	0.053**		0.033	0.039	0.035
HHSIZE	0.094	0.054	0.146	GSTOVE	-0.034	0.012	-0.041
	0.016**	0.015**	0.016**		0.027	0.031	0.026
HHSIZESQ	-0.005	-0.002	-0.008	ESTOVE	0.049	0.049	0.013
	0.001**	0.001*	0.001**		0.088	0.097	0.108
HHAGE	0.001	-0.001	0.000	FRIDGE	-0.059	-0.071	-0.064
	0.003	0.003	0.003		0.034+	0.035*	0.035+
HHAGESQ	-0.000	0.000	0.000	RADIO	0.018	0.031	0.020
	0.000	0.000	0.000		0.027	0.029	0.026
DISABLE	-0.012	-0.013	-0.037	STEREO	-0.061	-0.142	-0.086
	0.063	0.065	0.076		0.055	0.071*	0.063
SINGLEHH	-0.095	-0.112	-0.074	VIDEO	-0.058	-0.006	-0.074
	0.028**	0.029**	0.028**		0.051	0.041	0.056
URBAN	0.012	0.018	0.000	WASHMACH	-0.163	-0.002	-0.146
	0.052	0.053	0.052		0.151	0.089	0.159
HHINSUR	-0.309	-0.349	-0.214	TV	0.001	-0.025	-0.006
	0.147*	0.158*	0.150		0.033	0.034	0.032
REMITTANCE	-0.036	-0.060	-0.021	VEHICLES	0.025	0.078	0.054
	0.036	0.037	0.035		0.068	0.044+	0.048
FOSTERIN	0.038	-0.006	0.016	URBHINSU	0.069	0.084	0.092
	0.034	0.037	0.039		0.046	0.040*	0.022**
SUPPORT	0.068	0.087	0.080	URBREMIT	0.032	0.002	-0.003
	0.027*	0.028**	0.027**		0.041	0.051	0.050
ROOMS	0.035	0.002	0.039	URBFOSTER	-0.082	-0.039	-0.083
	0.023	0.024	0.023+		0.066	0.056	0.068
ROOMSQ	-0.004	-0.001	-0.005	URBSUPPT	-0.023	-0.061	-0.074
	0.002+	0.003	0.002+		0.054	0.066	0.066
WATER	-0.003	-0.020	0.005	URBWATER	0.001	0.044	-0.071
	0.031	0.032	0.031		0.056	0.047	0.075
TENURE	-0.016	-0.015	-0.033	URBTENURE	0.001	-0.017	0.008
	0.033	0.033	0.033		0.051	0.058	0.050
TELEPH	-0.049	-0.051	-0.078	URBTELE	-0.007	0.013	0.062
	0.044	0.043	0.047+		0.057	0.057	0.058
LIGHTING	0.036	0.021	0.005	URBLIGHT	0.081	0.106	0.073
	0.036	0.040	0.039		0.028**	0.024**	0.028**
SHRKITCH	0.012	0.020	0.014	URBSHTCH	-0.082	-0.156	-0.044
	0.035	0.038	0.035		0.072	0.091+	0.062
BASEDUC	-0.075	-0.038	-0.062				
	0.042+	0.050	0.045	Number of Obs.	795	795	795
SECEDUC	-0.140	-0.113	-0.084	Pseudo R²	0.28	0.25	0.33
	0.080+	0.076	0.073	Wald Chi²	168.3	174.7	182.8
SERVWORK	0.012	0.015	-0.012	Prob>Chi²	0.000	0.000	0.000
	0.026	0.027	0.028	Log likelihood	-274.9	-284.1	-272.4
AGRIWORK	0.077	0.073	0.066				
	0.025**	0.027**	0.025**				

Notes to tables 4a–4b: (1) Models 1, 2 and 3 reflect alternative assumptions of α = 0.15, 0.3 and 0.0 respectively; (2) robust standard errors are reported; (3) +,* and ** indicate significance at 10 per cent, 5 percent and 1 per cent levels respectively; (4) both the Pearson chi-square and Mosmer-Lemeshow goodness-of-fit tests suggest that the models fit reasonably well.

Appendix 4b Probit Marginal and Impact Effects: The Probability of Being Unanimously Poor (Objective Estimates, 1999)

	(1)	(2)	(3)		(1)	(2)	(3)
GENDER	0.059	0.089	0.058	SERVWORK	−0.023	−0.035	−0.002
	0.026*	0.031**	0.026*		0.025	0.028	0.023
CHIDEPEND	0.013	0.006	0.009	AGRIWORK	0.002	−0.011	0.009
	0.014	0.016	0.014		0.023	0.026	0.023
OLDDEPEND	−0.028	−0.023	−0.034	PERUEMP	0.110	0.081	0.106
	0.024	0.025	0.025		0.047*	0.050	0.048*
HHSIZE	0.013	0.042	−0.001	SEWMACH	−0.037	−0.054	−0.051
	0.015	0.017*	0.014		0.043	0.048	0.044
HHSIZESQ	−0.001	−0.003	0.001	GSTOVE	−0.036	−0.032	−0.047
	0.001	0.002+	0.001		0.024	0.024	0.025+
HHAGE	0.001	0.002	0.001	FRIDGE	−0.039	−0.027	−0.033
	0.002	0.003	0.003		0.027	0.028	0.026
HHAGESQ	0.000	0.000	0.000	RADIO	−0.005	0.008	0.004
	0.000	0.000	0.000		0.022	0.025	0.024
DISABLE	0.066	0.073	0.061	STEREO	−0.013	−0.016	−0.003
	0.015**	0.017**	0.018**		0.038	0.045	0.035
SINGLEHH	0.225	0.236	0.254	VIDEO	0.007	0.015	−0.031
	0.027**	0.026**	0.028**		0.026	0.028	0.033
PARTNER	−0.008	0.011	0.021	WASHMACH	−0.016	−0.023	−0.001
	0.057	0.056	0.035		0.063	0.076	0.056
URBAN	−0.001	−0.044	0.016	TV	0.044	0.020	0.042
	0.044	0.055	0.044		0.029	0.029	0.032
HHINSUR	0.034	−0.031	−0.039	VEHICLES	−0.062	−0.058	−0.087
	0.051	0.114	0.094		0.071	0.072	0.072
REMITTANCE	−0.020	−0.050	−0.044	URBHINSU	−0.378	−0.159	−0.159
	0.027	0.031	0.029		0.289	0.228	0.185
FOSTERIN	−0.006	−0.006	0.003	URBREMIT	−0.005	0.012	0.041
	0.026	0.029	0.026		0.040	0.037	0.026
SUPPORT	0.036	0.041	0.036	URBFOSTER	0.042	0.054	0.039
	0.022	0.023+	0.023		0.026	0.026*	0.028
ROOMS	−0.049	−0.058	−0.045	URBSUPPT	0.022	0.021	−0.005
	0.020*	0.021**	0.022*		0.032	0.036	0.043
ROOMSQ	0.002	0.002	0.001	URBWATER	0.014	0.034	0.013
	0.002	0.002	0.002		0.037	0.032	0.037
WATER	0.007	−0.007	0.011	URBTENURE	−0.010	0.001	−0.019
	0.025	0.027	0.025		0.040	0.040	0.044
TENURE	0.013	−0.014	0.018	URBTELE	−0.046	−0.057	−0.057
	0.025	0.026	0.026		0.046	0.052	0.047
TELEPH	−0.025	−0.009	−0.028	URBLIGHT	0.007	0.015	−0.036
	0.032	0.037	0.032		0.042	0.043	0.061
LIGHTING	0.049	0.060	0.051	URBSHTCH	−0.151	−0.042	−0.210
	0.027+	0.028*	0.028+		0.123	0.076	0.148
SHRKITCH	0.081	0.067	0.082				
	0.024**	0.027*	0.025**	Number of Obs.	800	798	802
BASEDUC	−0.047	−0.067	−0.083	Pseudo R²	0.35	0.33	0.39
	0.037	0.037+	0.032**	Wald Chi²	218.4	191.1	232.3
SECEDUC	−0.035	−0.110	−0.114	Prob>Chi²	0.000	0.000	0.000
	0.070	0.098	0.100	Log likelihood	−253.6	−259.9	−254.2

Probit Marginal and Impact Effects

Appendix 5a   Probit Marginal and Impact Effects: The Probability of Being Unanimously Poor (Subjective Self-Classification, 1997)

	(1)	(2)	(3)		(1)	(2)	(3)
GENDER	−0.020	−0.009	−0.025	SERVWORK	0.005	−0.002	0.006
	0.015	0.014	0.013*		0.009	0.010	0.005
CHIDEPEND	−0.004	0.001	−0.001	AGRIWORK	0.004	−0.013	0.012
	0.006	0.006	0.004		0.013	0.019	0.007+
OLDDEPEND	0.007	0.016	−0.004	PERUEMP	0.035	0.039	0.028
	0.019	0.019	0.014		0.020+	0.021+	0.014*
HHSIZE	0.011	−0.017	0.017	SEWMACH	0.001	0.001	0.000
	0.005*	0.006**	0.004**		0.012	0.012	0.008
HHSIZESQ	−0.001	0.001	−0.001	GSTOVE	−0.012	−0.017	−0.013
	0.000+	0.000*	0.000**		0.011	0.012	0.006*
HHAGE	−0.002	−0.002	−0.002	FRIDGE	−0.026	−0.019	−0.008
	0.001+	0.001	0.001*		0.014+	0.013	0.008
HHAGESQ	0.000	0.000	0.000	RADIO	−0.009	−0.014	−0.004
	0.000*	0.000	0.000**		0.009	0.010	0.006
DISABLE	0.027	0.038		STEREO	−0.021	−0.022	−0.020
	0.010**	0.008**			0.021	0.020	0.017
SINGLEHH	−0.054	−0.049	−0.068	VIDEO	0.001	−0.027	0.006
	0.024*	0.022*	0.030*		0.013	0.018	0.007
PARTNER	0.026	0.006	−0.008	WASHMACH	0.008	0.021	−0.018
	0.011*	0.021	0.021		0.030	0.019	0.043
URBAN	−0.009	−0.026	0.000	TV	0.023	0.004	0.009
	0.023	0.026	0.013		0.013+	0.013	0.008
HHINSUR	−0.086	−0.034	−0.029	VEHICLES	−0.036	−0.187	−0.039
	0.054	0.036	0.027		0.032	0.060**	0.033
REMITTANCE	−0.018	−0.006	−0.012	URBHINSU	0.020	0.006	0.005
	0.015	0.015	0.010		0.013	0.024	0.012
FOSTERIN	−0.026	−0.043	−0.027	URBREMIT	0.009	−0.003	0.011
	0.019	0.021*	0.016+		0.014	0.020	0.007+
SUPPORT	0.008	−0.017	0.009	URBFOSTER	0.006	0.010	−0.003
	0.013	0.018	0.007		0.016	0.016	0.013
ROOMS	0.013	0.008	0.012	URBSUPP	0.001	0.004	−0.008
	0.009	0.010	0.007+		0.020	0.019	0.017
ROOMSQ	−0.001	−0.000	−0.001	URBWATER	0.010	0.002	0.012
	0.001	0.001	0.001		0.021	0.032	0.008
WATER	0.025	0.038	0.007	URBTENURE	0.014	0.016	0.019
	0.013+	0.015*	0.008		0.015	0.016	0.007**
TENURE	0.016	0.002	0.002	URBTELE	−0.030	−0.033	−0.045
	0.015	0.016	0.009		0.031	0.034	0.037
TELEPH	−0.020	−0.011	−0.012	URBLIGHT	0.014	0.018	0.001
	0.019	0.019	0.014		0.017	0.020	0.013
LIGHTING	0.013	0.006	0.004	URBSHTCH	0.005	0.028	0.007
	0.016	0.021	0.009		0.022	0.013*	0.010
SHRKITCH	−0.030	−0.061	−0.028				
	0.032	0.047	0.023	Number of obs.	1328	1328	1328
BASICED	0.010	0.016	0.005	Pseudo R²	0.240	0.280	0.320
	0.016	0.017	0.010	Wald Chi²	155.3	178.2	155.6
SECEDUC	0.000	−0.005	−0.003	Prob>Chi²	0.000	0.000	0.000
	0.015	0.016	0.010	Log likelihood	−274.9	−295.3	−231.9

Appendix 5b Probit Marginal and Impact Effects: The Probability of Being Unanimously Poor (Objective Estimates, 1997)

	(1)	(2)	(3)		(1)	(2)	(3)
GENDER	0.003	0.004	0.004	SERVWORK	−0.002	−0.001	−0.002
	0.002	0.004	0.002+		0.002	0.002	0.002
CHIDEPEND	0.002	0.000	0.003	AGRIWORK	−0.001	0.000	−0.001
	0.002	0.001	0.002+		0.001	0.001	0.002
OLDDEPEND	−0.001	−0.001	−0.002	PERUEMP	−0.001	0.000	0.000
	0.001	0.002	0.001		0.002	0.002	0.002
HHSIZE	0.005	0.004	0.003	SEWMACH	0.001	0.000	0.001
	0.003+	0.005	0.002*		0.001	0.001	0.001
HHSIZESQ	0.000	0.000	0.000	GSTOVE	−0.001	−0.001	0.000
	0.000	0.000	0.000+		0.001	0.001	0.001
HHAGE	0.000	0.000	0.000	ESTOVE	−0.016	−0.027	−0.007
	0.000	0.000	0.000		0.029	0.036	0.016
HHAGESQ	0.000	0.000	0.000	FRIDGE	−0.005	−0.002	−0.004
	0.000	0.000	0.000		0.003	0.003	0.002+
DISABLE	−0.001	0.000	0.000	RADIO	0.000	0.000	−0.001
	0.003	0.001	0.002		0.001	0.001	0.001
SINGLEHH	0.006	0.005	0.007	STEREO	0.001	0.000	−0.001
	0.003+	0.005	0.003*		0.001	0.001	0.002
PARTNER	−0.002	−0.001	0.001	VIDEO	0.000	0.000	−0.001
	0.003	0.002	0.001		0.001	0.001	0.002
URBAN	−0.003	−0.001	−0.004	WASHMACH	−0.011	−0.008	−0.011
	0.003	0.002	0.004		0.015	0.014	0.015
HHINSUR	−0.013	−0.007	−0.004	TV	0.000	0.000	−0.001
	0.016	0.011	0.006		0.001	0.001	0.001
REMITTANCE	−0.002	−0.001	−0.003	VEHICLES	−0.006	−0.001	−0.006
	0.002	0.001	0.002		0.006	0.002	0.007
FOSTERIN	0.003	0.002	0.002	URBHINSU	0.001	0.001	−0.002
	0.002+	0.002	0.001		0.001	0.001	0.005
SUPPORT	−0.002	−0.001	−0.002	URBREMIT	0.000	−0.001	0.001
	0.002	0.001	0.002		0.001	0.003	0.001
ROOMS	−0.003	−0.002	−0.005	URBFOSTER	−0.027	−0.012	−0.004
	0.002+	0.003	0.002*		0.028	0.016	0.007
ROOMSQ	0.000	0.000	0.000	URBSUPP	0.001	0.001	0.001
	0.000	0.000	0.000+		0.001	0.001	0.001
WATER	−0.001	−0.001	−0.001	URBWATER	0.000	0.000	0.000
	0.001	0.002	0.002		0.002	0.001	0.002
TENURE	−0.002	−0.001	0.001	URBTENURE	0.001	0.001	0.002
	0.001	0.001	0.002		0.001	0.001	0.001
TELEPH	0.001	0.000	0.000	URBTELE	−0.004	−0.002	−0.001
	0.001	0.001	0.001		0.006	0.004	0.003
LIGHTING	−0.002	0.001	0.001	URBLIGHT	0.002	0.000	0.000
	0.002	0.001	0.002		0.001	0.001	0.003
SHRKITCH	0.001	0.001	0.011	URBSHTCH	−0.008	−0.001	−0.997
	0.001	0.001	0.004*		0.015	0.003	0.001**
BELBASED	0.002	0.001	0.002				
	0.001	0.001	0.001+	Number of Obs.	1281	1282	1277
BASICED	0.007	0.004	0.005	Pseudo R^2	0.489	0.487	0.461
	0.008	0.006	0.006	Wald Chi^2	198.1	221.7	302.3
SECEDUC	0.002	0.001	0.003	Prob>Chi^2	0.000	0.000	0.000
	0.002	0.002	0.002	Log likelihood	−179.5	−204.5	−176.9

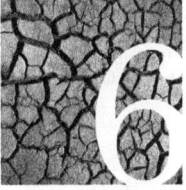

Probit Marginal and Impact Effects

Appendix 6a Probit Marginal and Impact Effects: The Probability of Being Unanimously Poor (Subjective Self-Classification, 1993)

	(1)	(2)	(3)		(1)	(2)	(3)
GENDER	−0.018	−0.015	−0.028	SECEDUC	0.032	0.051	0.021
	0.017	0.022	0.021		0.018+	0.026*	0.025
CHIDEPEND	−0.035	−0.043	−0.041	SERVWORK	−0.026	−0.014	−0.019
	0.010**	0.013**	0.010**		0.021	0.025	0.021
OLDDEPEND	0.051	0.044	0.057	AGRIWORK	−0.015	−0.017	0.004
	0.026+	0.035	0.030+		0.020	0.027	0.019
HHSIZE	−0.038	−0.069	−0.014	PERUEMP	−0.005	−0.014	−0.028
	0.010**	0.014**	0.010		0.025	0.034	0.027
HHSIZESQ	0.002	0.003	0.001	SEWMACH	−0.046	−0.040	−0.027
	0.001**	0.001**	0.001		0.038	0.042	0.035
HHAGE	−0.001	−0.005	0.000	GSTOVE	−0.004	−0.031	−0.002
	0.003	0.004	0.003		0.016	0.026	0.017
HHAGESQ	0.000	0.000	0.000	FRIDGE	−0.010	−0.004	0.020
	0.000	0.000	0.000		0.022	0.027	0.017
DISABLE	0.030	0.047	0.012	RADIO	−0.035	−0.056	−0.038
	0.013*	0.016**	0.027		0.016*	0.020**	0.016*
SINGLEHH	−0.140	−0.196	−0.137	STEREO	−0.028	0.000	−0.061
	0.056*	0.069**	0.056*		0.060	0.066	0.091
PARTNER	−0.007	0.020	−0.009	VIDEO	−0.002	0.000	−0.080
	0.021	0.022	0.022		0.030	0.039	0.070
URBAN	0.013	0.060	0.059	TV	0.008	−0.015	−0.002
	0.043	0.056	0.043		0.018	0.030	0.022
HHINSUR	0.054	−0.736	0.021	VEHICLES	−0.350	-	−0.002
	0.155	0.169**	0.042		0.248	-	0.059
REMITTANCE	0.000	−0.007	−0.004	URBHINSU	−0.155	0.052	−0.198
	0.017	0.025	0.019		0.320	0.015**	0.371
FOSTERIN	0.025	0.041	0.035	URBREMIT	−0.009	−0.040	−0.007
	0.014+	0.020*	0.015*		0.034	0.058	0.037
SUPPORT	0.002	0.036	−0.001	URBFOSTER	−0.024	−0.064	−0.086
	0.019	0.021+	0.021		0.046	0.073	0.082
ROOMS	0.009	−0.006	0.008	URBSUPP	0.013	−0.082	−0.007
	0.014	0.020	0.016		0.033	0.096	0.047
ROOMSQ	0.000	0.002	−0.001	URBWATER	0.012	−0.040	−0.012
	0.001	0.002	0.002		0.028	0.066	0.047
WATER	0.018	0.038	−0.010	URBTENURE	−0.044	−0.069	−0.102
	0.023	0.034	0.023		0.060	0.084	0.084
TENURE	0.061	0.034	0.050	URBTELE	0.028	−0.418	0.039
	0.060	0.063	0.053		0.026	0.361	0.010**
TELEPH	−0.142	0.038	−0.379	URBLIGHT	0.047	0.076	0.034
	0.255	0.031	0.390		0.016**	0.022**	0.021+
LIGHTING	0.004	−0.027	0.001	URBSHTCH	0.018	0.007	−0.019
	0.022	0.028	0.026		0.035	0.058	0.072
SHRKITCH	−0.020	−0.050	−0.003				
	0.057	0.079	0.045	Number of Obs.	532	532	532
BELBASED	0.002	0.053	0.015	Pseudo R^2	0.339	0.398	0.276
	0.048	0.016**	0.037	Wald Chi^2	140	158.2	109.1
BASICED	0.023	0.091	0.014	Prob>Chi^2	0.000	0.000	0.000
	0.045	0.076	0.039	Log likelihood	−133.2	−155.7	−116.8

Appendix 6b Probit Marginal and Impact Effects: The Probability of Being Unanimously Poor (Objective Estimates, 1993)

	(1)	(2)	(3)		(1)	(2)	(3)
GENDER	0.028	0.030	0.014	SECEDUC	0.027	0.051	0.016
	0.018	0.027	0.011		0.028	0.027+	0.015
CHIDEPEND	0.072	0.058	0.058	SERVWORK	−0.013	−0.029	−0.021
	0.019**	0.023*	0.015**		0.022	0.033	0.016
OLDDEPEND	0.018	0.016	−0.002	AGRIWORK	−0.028	−0.062	−0.017
	0.017	0.022	0.011		0.022	0.031*	0.015
HHSIZE	0.016	0.082	−0.009	PERUEMP	0.055	0.085	0.055
	0.012	0.021**	0.007		0.034	0.048+	0.024*
HHSIZESQ	0.000	−0.003	0.001	SEWMACH	0.013	−0.006	0.001
	0.001	0.002*	0.001		0.019	0.039	0.014
HHAGE	0.007	0.008	0.003	GSTOVE	−0.008	−0.042	−0.006
	0.003**	0.003*	0.002+		0.018	0.033	0.011
HHAGESQ	0.000	0.000	0.000	FRIDGE	0.000	−0.037	0.001
	0.000*	0.000+	0.000		0.022	0.040	0.012
DISABLE	0.019	0.037		RADIO	−0.002	−0.017	0.002
	0.016	0.018*			0.015	0.019	0.010
SINHLEHH	0.032	0.030	0.019	STEREO	−0.075	−0.028	0.000
	0.015*	0.023	0.009*		0.120	0.127	0.032
PARTNER	−0.031	−0.019	0.012	VIDEO	0.007	−0.024	0.003
	0.035	0.042	0.009		0.032	0.071	0.018
URBAN	−0.027	−0.029	0.004	TV	−0.041	−0.082	−0.025
	0.051	0.067	0.036		0.028	0.041*	0.017
HHINSUR	0.041	0.059	0.022	URBHINSU	−0.968	−0.954	−0.984
	0.012**	0.014**	0.009*		0.009**	0.012**	0.007**
REMITTANCE	−0.028	−0.025	−0.001	URBREMITT	0.021	0.032	0.007
	0.023	0.030	0.011		0.019	0.025	0.016
FOSTERIN	−0.002	0.021	0.004	URBFOSTER	0.015	−0.147	0.004
	0.023	0.032	0.011		0.033	0.139	0.024
SUPPORT	−0.008	−0.001	−0.016	URBSUPP	0.041	0.039	0.025
	0.020	0.026	0.016		0.012**	0.022+	0.009**
ROOMS	−0.038	−0.022	−0.029	URBWATER	0.031	0.032	0.008
	0.016*	0.020	0.012*		0.016*	0.027	0.016
ROOMSQ	0.002	0.000	0.002	URBTENURE	−0.067	−0.044	−0.038
	0.002	0.002	0.001		0.067	0.069	0.061
WATER	−0.001	0.002	0.009	URBTELE	0.038	−0.943	0.020
	0.020	0.027	0.013		0.011**	0.019**	0.008*
TENURE	0.036	0.020	−0.010	URBLIGHT	0.013	−0.005	0.007
	0.043	0.050	0.016		0.025	0.041	0.014
TELEPH	−0.586	0.060	−0.399	URBSHTCH	0.032	0.060	−0.020
	0.322+	0.015**	0.243		0.016*	0.017**	0.054
LIGHTING	0.001	0.004	−0.009				
	0.022	0.029	0.014				
SHRKITCH	−0.038	−0.111	0.004				
	0.049	0.085	0.022	Number of Obs.	536	535	536
BELBASED	−0.048	−0.068	0.000	Pseudo R^2	0.32	0.41	0.31
	0.100	0.119	0.036	LR Chi^2	138.5	213.7	109.6
BASICED	−0.012	0.000	0.005	Prob>Chi^2	0.000	0.000	0.000
	0.035	0.051	0.028	Log Likelihood	−142.9	−155	−115.5

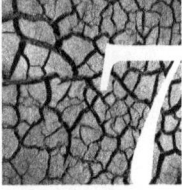

Multinomial Logit Marginal and Impact Effects

Appendix 7a Multinomial Logit Marginal and Impact Effects: The Probability of Being Incorrectly Poor, 1999

	(1)	(2)	(3)		(1)	(2)	(3)
CHIDEPEND	0.438	−0.017	−0.230	AGRIWORK	−0.894	−0.327	−0.095
	0.140***	0.123	0.171		0.332***	0.208	0.275
OLDDEPEND	−2.017	−0.397	0.470	PERUEMP	−0.566	−1.608	−1.255
	0.601***	0.329	0.287		0.428	0.400***	0.557**
HHSIZE	−0.795	−0.864	−0.144	SEWMACH	0.013	0.679	0.195
	0.140***	0.114***	0.165		0.374	0.250***	0.363
HHSIZESQ	0.045	0.047	0.013	GSTOVE	0.363	0.560	0.613
	0.011***	0.010***	0.014		0.288	0.213***	0.340*
HHAGE	−0.004	−0.028	−0.011	ESTOVE	−0.118	0.741	−4.435
	0.028	0.019	0.031		1.266	0.659	0.872***
HHAGESQ	0.000	0.000	0.000	FRIDGE	0.511	0.604	0.608
	0.000	0.000	0.000		0.278*	0.195***	0.300**
DISABLE	0.060	−0.402	−1.512	RADIO	−0.188	−0.257	0.286
	0.587	0.409	0.811*		0.246	0.175	0.284
SINGLEHH	0.621	−1.120	−3.153	STEREO	0.270	0.494	0.386
	0.264**	0.179***	0.417***		0.391	0.282*	0.400
PARTNER	−35.150	1.056	0.213	VIDEO	0.592	0.290	−0.187
	0.509***	0.461**	0.617		0.341*	0.246	0.338
URBAN	−0.308	−0.002	−0.027	WASHMACH	0.893	0.606	0.399
	0.489	0.335	0.556		0.709	0.585	0.703
HHINSUR	1.519	1.603	−0.109	TV	−0.185	0.019	−0.458
	0.590***	0.475***	0.845		0.310	0.225	0.345
REMITTANCE	0.456	0.233	0.237	VEHICLES	−0.091	1.567	0.234
	0.312	0.211	0.301		0.777	0.407***	0.522
FOSTERIN	−0.274	−0.092	−0.317	URHINSU	−0.828	−0.095	0.622
	0.365	0.251	0.347		0.883	0.604	1.051
SUPPORT	−0.547	−0.277	−0.445	URBREMMIT	−0.470	−0.288	−0.002
	0.321*	0.225	0.317		0.465	0.308	0.441
ROOMS	−0.372	0.387	0.696	URBFOSTER	0.858	−0.318	−0.243
	0.218*	0.157**	0.259***		0.472*	0.342	0.506
ROOMSQ	0.040	−0.013	−0.039	URBSUPPT	0.147	−0.327	−0.449
	0.023*	0.016	0.027		0.470	0.340	0.504
WATER	−0.209	−0.450	0.165	URBWATER	−0.067	−0.322	−0.054
	0.296	0.210**	0.299		0.568	0.398	0.489
TENURE	0.284	−0.104	−0.343	URBRENURE	0.188	0.224	0.213
	0.317	0.218	0.327		0.492	0.323	0.448
TELEPH	0.182	0.849	0.601	URBTELE	0.178	0.700	0.654
	0.386	0.265***	0.379		0.532	0.381*	0.552
LIGHTING	−0.315	−0.511	−0.609	URBLIGHT	−1.234	−0.206	0.118
	0.402	0.287*	0.440		0.586**	0.396	0.604
SHRKITCH	−0.071	−0.529	−1.918	URBSHTCH	0.791	0.839	1.990
	0.348	0.276*	0.782**		0.498	0.380**	0.925**
BASEDUC	0.746	−0.116	0.618	Constant	0.128	1.936	−2.896
	0.485	0.328	0.537		0.827	0.555***	0.939***
SECEDUC	0.908	0.282	0.240				
	0.481*	0.333	0.572	Observations	1857	1857	1857
SERVWORK	−0.185	0.081	0.279	Pseudo R^2			0.355
	0.245	0.171	0.255	Log pseudo likelihood			−1349.2

Notes: (1) Models 1, 2 and 3 are for the "incorrectly" poor, non-poor correct and "incorrectly" not poor; the base category is unanimously poor; (2) robust standard errors are reported; (3) *,** and *** indicate significant at 10 per cent, 5 per cent and 1 per cent respectively.

Appendix 7b Multinomial Logit Marginal and Impact Effects: The Probability of Being Incorrectly Poor, 1997

	(1)	(2)	(3)
GENDER	0.362	-0.020	-1.070
	0.414	0.272	0.414***
CHIDEPEND	0.156	-0.161	-1.133
	0.155	0.187	0.628*
OLDDEPEND	-0.331	-0.259	0.238
	0.524	0.307	0.344
HHSIZE	-0.276	-1.247	-1.060
	0.135**	0.119***	0.465**
HHSIZESQ	0.014	0.056	-0.012
	0.009	0.008***	0.080
HHAGE	0.063	-0.012	0.042
	0.038*	0.022	0.040
HHAGESQ	-0.001	0.000	-0.001
	0.001**	0.000	0.000
DISABLE	-0.883	-0.969	0.844
	1.031	0.631	0.581
SINGLEHH	1.058	-0.712	-2.271
	0.421**	0.298**	0.467***
PARTNER	-0.989	0.388	0.271
	0.900	0.330	0.516
URBAN	0.226	0.659	1.299
	0.585	0.352*	0.693*
HHINSUR	1.245	1.302	1.585
	0.501**	0.378***	0.835*
REMITTANCE	0.603	0.289	0.539
	0.349*	0.260	0.364
FOSTERIN	0.664	-0.290	-1.436
	0.395*	0.365	0.749*
SUPPORT	-0.279	-0.395	0.762
	0.401	0.311	0.390*
ROOMS	-0.530	0.314	1.184
	0.225**	0.157**	0.232***
ROOMSQ	0.055	0.005	-0.043
	0.021***	0.015	0.020**
WATER	-0.716	-0.241	0.337
	0.371*	0.250	0.389
TENURE	-0.239	0.063	0.510
	0.412	0.267	0.459
TELEPH	0.418	0.211	0.185
	0.393	0.318	0.526
LIGHTING	-0.516	-0.372	0.438
	0.570	0.340	0.537
SHRKITCH	0.476	-0.495	-0.545
	0.584	0.425	1.104
BASEDUC	-0.049	-1.010	-0.281
	0.397	0.288***	0.502
SECEDUC	0.132	-0.398	-0.071
	0.380	0.267	0.531
SERVWORK	-0.041	0.039	0.508
	0.256	0.173	0.312

	(1)	(2)	(3)
AGRIWORK	-0.103	-0.474	0.617
	0.450	0.277*	0.381
PERUEMP	-0.980	-0.207	0.175
	0.529*	0.387	0.640
SEWMACH	0.005	-0.186	-0.068
	0.337	0.241	0.374
GSTOVE	0.307	0.448	-0.039
	0.328	0.249*	0.406
ESTOVE	-29.586	1.195	0.485
	0.843***	0.768	1.382
FRIDGE	0.717	0.211	1.120
	0.321**	0.221	0.383***
RADIO	0.154	0.062	0.132
	0.276	0.187	0.295
STEREO	0.444	0.403	-0.082
	0.368	0.254	0.441
VIDEO	0.073	0.598	-0.123
	0.319	0.220***	0.389
WASHMACH	0.143	1.158	1.232
	0.903	0.467**	0.621**
TV	-0.756	0.081	0.338
	0.321**	0.225	0.392
VEHICLES	0.704	1.611	0.820
	0.471	0.281***	0.508
URBHINSU	-0.549	0.154	-1.047
	0.600	0.447	0.958
URBREMITT	-0.405	0.078	-0.595
	0.469	0.342	0.524
URBFOSTER	-0.149	0.159	1.389
	0.486	0.437	0.988
URBSUPP	-0.038	0.120	-0.577
	0.536	0.386	0.554
URBWATER	-0.157	-0.213	-0.244
	0.879	0.498	0.739
URBRENURE	-0.401	-0.386	-0.748
	0.540	0.344	0.620
URBTELE	0.651	0.778	0.689
	0.516	0.385**	0.678
URBLIGHT	-0.333	-1.196	-0.990
	0.760	0.527**	0.749
URBSHTCH	0.000	0.217	0.972
	0.682	0.488	1.221
Constant	-2.505	1.322	-4.151
	0.986**	0.617**	1.308***
Observations	1964	1964	1964
Pseudo R^2			0.401
Log pseudo likelihood			-1124.1

Notes: (1) Models 1, 2 and 3 are for the "incorrectly" poor, non-poor correct and "incorrectly" not poor; the base category is unanimously poor; (2) robust standard errors in parentheses; (3) *,** and *** indicate significant at 10 per cent, 5 per cent and 1 per cent respectively.

Appendix 7c Multinomial Logit Marginal and Impact Effects: The Probability of Being Incorrectly Poor, 1993

	(1)	(2)	(3)		(1)	(2)	(3)
GENDER	0.718	0.029	−0.517	AGRIWORK	0.580	−0.021	0.385
	0.396*	0.179	0.371		0.428	0.193	0.365
CHIDEPEND	0.730	−0.718	−1.943	PERUEMP	0.418	−0.927	−1.762
	0.183***	0.119***	0.460***		0.602	0.313***	0.863**
OLDDEPEND	−1.088	−0.215	−0.369	SEWMACH	0.472	0.200	0.178
	0.754	0.262	0.476		0.467	0.268	0.517
HHSIZE	1.049	−0.467	−0.139	GSTOVE	0.167	0.731	−0.124
	0.234***	0.097***	0.255		0.364	0.181***	0.340
HHSIZESQ	−0.046	0.018	−0.016	ESTOVE	0.384	31.700	−0.647
	0.014***	0.007**	0.024		1.362	0.684***	0.809
HHAGE	−0.015	−0.028	−0.116	FRIDGE	0.019	0.435	0.286
	0.074	0.029	0.050**		0.445	0.220**	0.401
HHAGESQ	0.000	−0.000	0.001	RADIO	0.816	0.381	0.120
	0.001	0.000	0.000**		0.472*	0.161**	0.326
DISABLE	−0.866	−1.561	−0.397	STEREO	0.408	0.615	0.770
	0.841	0.433***	0.631		0.817	0.543	0.972
SINGLEHH	1.905	0.039	−0.987	VIDEO	−0.165	0.209	−0.862
	0.530***	0.229	0.488**		0.585	0.347	0.818
PARTNER	0.489	0.491	0.267	WASHMACH	−0.451	29.855	−0.684
	0.453	0.201**	0.447		0.960	0.646***	0.997
URBAN	−0.299	−0.332	−0.879	TV	−0.065	0.448	0.593
	0.986	0.518	0.944		0.472	0.209**	0.407
HHINSUR	1.176	1.324	−19.546	VEHICLES	2.674	2.122	−30.267
	1.152	0.758*	1.031***		1.189**	1.037**	1.061***
REMITTANCE	0.240	−0.065	0.366	URBHINSU	−0.082	0.773	21.890
	0.382	0.215	0.373		1.582	1.016	0.000
FOSTERIN	−0.738	−0.245	−0.185	URBREMITT	0.202	0.416	−0.065
	0.501	0.239	0.509		0.685	0.358	0.684
SUPPORT	0.158	0.194	−0.086	URBFOSTIN	0.906	0.816	−0.177
	0.443	0.220	0.390		0.743	0.385**	1.159
ROOMS	−0.436	0.147	1.033	URBSUPP	−1.283	−0.638	−1.308
	0.413	0.202	0.545*		1.350	0.359*	0.882
ROOMSQ	0.063	0.017	−0.100	URBWATER	−0.088	−0.026	−0.076
	0.055	0.029	0.085		0.957	0.345	0.666
WATER	−0.535	−0.483	−0.456	URBTRENURE	0.909	0.298	1.175
	0.471	0.217**	0.403		0.919	0.460	0.827
TENURE	−0.866	−0.293	−1.127	URBTELE	−1.222	−1.110	−1.538
	0.624	0.357	0.607*		1.681	1.172	1.821
TELEPH	1.835	2.435	1.586	URBLIGHT	−2.105	−0.276	−0.169
	1.400	1.042**	1.582		0.827**	0.321	0.629
LIGHTING	−0.110	−0.099	−0.088	URBSHTCH	0.926	−0.216	−0.154
	0.543	0.243	0.451		0.958	0.365	0.803
SHRKITCH	0.112	−0.142	0.376	Constant	−6.465	3.335	1.811
	0.740	0.232	0.475		2.302***	0.896***	1.860
BASEDUC	−0.229	0.266	1.062				
	0.563	0.296	0.830				
SECEDUC	−0.926	−0.063	0.373				
	0.670	0.320	0.868	Observations	1926	1926	1926
SERVWORK	0.754	0.342	−0.044	Pseudo R²			0.352
	0.383**	0.176*	0.395	Log pseudo likelihood			−1046

Notes: (1) Models 1, 2 and 3 are for the "incorrectly" poor, non-poor correct and "incorrectly" not poor; the base category is unanimously poor; (2) robust standard errors in parentheses; (3) *,** and *** indicate significant at 10 per cent, 5 per cent and 1 per cent respectively.

Notes

Chapter 1

1. Analysis of the impact of macroeconomic adjustment on the poor is difficult due to the complexities of adjustments within the household, with possible important lags, feedbacks and substitutions.
2. A work that is still relevant having set the foundation for future poverty studies and in facilitating an understanding of the dynamics of social stratification and mobility in the Caribbean.
3. Gordon (1987, 30–32) argues that Jamaicans whose parents were agricultural labourers, small farmers, domestics and unskilled manual workers had virtually no chance of ending up at the top of the middle class strata despite the expansion of the educational system. The inequality of opportunities is less sharp, though the gap between the middle strata, as a whole, and the mass of working class remains large, with the children of agricultural labourers and small farmers having the worst overall chance of upward mobility. However, individuals from the middle strata were also more likely to remain in the middle strata.
4. See Easterlin (1995), Clark and Oswald (1994), Blanchflower and Oswald (2004), and Di Tella, MacCulloch and Oswald (2003).
5. The literature on the dynamics of poverty makes a distinction between the chronic and transitory poor. Jalan and Ravallion (2000) define chronic and transitory poverty, by focusing on the contribution of inter-temporal variability in living standards to poverty (see Jalan and Ravallion 2000; and McCulloch and Baulch 2000 for elaboration). Early references in the literature identified the chronic poor as those individuals or households consuming below a poverty line normally equivalent to the cost of the basic nutritional food requirements (Laderchi 1997). But the more recent literature on the dynamics of poverty uses the term "chronic poor" to identify those households who are always poor. Using data for thirteen different panels in ten different countries, Baulch and Hoddinott (2000) show that the percentage of households that

experience poverty for one to two time periods was almost always greater than the percentage of those households characterized as always poor. This points to the importance of distinguishing between the chronic and transitory poor and of the indicators used to identify and target them. However, this issue is not addressed in this text.

6. Some individuals may become poor due to inherent vulnerabilities such as disability or region of residence. As such, certain combinations of vulnerabilities may be strongly correlated with poverty but the concepts are not the same. Poverty relates to deprivation, while vulnerability is a function of risks, shocks and internal defencelessness (Lok-Dessallien 2000). McCulloch and Calandrino (2002) define vulnerability as the probability of a household falling below the poverty line in any given year.

7. Although income data are collected in the Jamaica Labour Force Survey by the Statistical Institute of Jamaica, at best it is reported to be unreliable and the practice has been to use JSLC survey in which consumption data are collected. Theoretical and practical arguments are identified by Deaton (1997), Lipton and Ravallion (1995), and Ravallion (1992) in favour of the use of consumption to estimate poverty. They argue that consumption is a more stable variable and more accurately measured in the context of developing countries. This will be reflected in falling consumption for those who cannot smooth, which correctly indicates lower welfare. Notwithstanding this, there are also problems related to the use of consumption. For instance, different households may face different constraints on their consumption smoothing behaviour, and changes in total consumption may affect the welfare of different household members in different ways and in different directions (Lipton and Ravallion 1995).

8. While the absolute threshold is fixed at a point in time and updated solely for price changes, relative poverty lines are updated for changes in real consumption (Citro and Michael 1995).

9. These welfarist measures may also be expressed in terms of happiness or the satisfaction of desires or preferences.

10. This is supported by Di Tella, MacCulloch and Oswald (2003) using data for the European Union and the United States, showing that marriage and high income are associated with high well-being scores.

11. The participatory approach has evolved over the past three decades, first being related to rural development and basic needs strategies, then being associated with grassroots self-reliance and self-help, along with empowerment and good governance.

12. The participatory approach has uncovered a broad range of variables that influence people's sense of ill-being. However, see Chambers (1997) for an

outline of a number of problems associated with the use of this technique, and of which the researcher must be conscious.

13. "It is assumed instead that the economist knows the answer on the basis of objective data on incomes and prices" (Ravallion and Lokshin 1999, 2).

14. Yet poverty should accord with what is socially expected to be the minimum requirements in society.

15. The presumption is that consumption/income is highly correlated with other socio-economic variables so that it suffices alone as an adequate indicator.

16. Data quality checks and cleaning were performed by the Statistical Institute of Jamaica. The former initially involved entry and re-entry of the data, but increasingly, given their experience, the Statistical Institute has relied on checking a sample of the data. This is also based on high levels of supervision of the fieldwork and clear instructions to field staff. On both fronts these quality control initiatives are commendable. In addition, checks are also conducted for univariate and multivariate outliers and appropriate action taken if an error is detected.

17. Consumption data in the JSLC covers daily expenses, meals away from home, food and non-food expenses, and non-consumption. These categories have remained unchanged over the life of the JSLC. However, the latter group is not included in our analysis of consumption expenditure. For each item of consumption, households are asked for a short and long period of recall, and the two estimates are weighted in arriving at the annual estimate for the particular item.

18. Includes tobacco products, reading materials, gardening and horticulture, telephone and flowers.

19. The JSLC data sets suffered from both random and non-random missing data, and given the relatively small size of the data set, all the observations have been retained. Several methods were employed to address the problem of missing data. Depending on the particular case, missing data were either assigned zero, values were assigned "intelligently", the area mean was used for the relevant variables or by modelling, for example, asset ownership for each asset separately, using a probit regression only for those households who had reported and then fitted values were used to assign a value to each of the non-reporting households.

20. The urban-rural divide is generally equal but urban is divided into the KMA and other towns.

21. An issue that must also be considered is the accuracy of the frame, which invariably excludes homeless people and those living in institutions. The JSLC frame is based on the population census and is updated between censuses to account for changes in the population.

Chapter 2

1. The official estimate (JSLC method) suggests that the percentage of poor households declined from 17.7 per cent in 1993 to 11.9 and 11.4 per cent in 1997 and 1999, respectively, and the corresponding per-adult equivalent poverty lines are US$1.8, US$2.6 and US$2.7, respectively. On the other hand, 6.8 per cent, 5.6 per cent and 5.2 per cent of households could not afford the basic food requirements and would therefore be food poor. The corresponding lines are US$1.05, US$1.6 and US$1.7, respectively, and are more consistent with the World Bank standard of one United States dollar a day. The challenge of meeting the Millennium Development Goals, in terms of reducing the poverty headcount by half in 2015, is therefore seen as attainable, and this is true for most Caribbean countries. The level of poverty in Jamaica compares favourably with one-off estimates for St. Lucia (18.7 per cent in 1995), Dominica (29.0 per cent), and Trinidad and Tobago (18.5 per cent in 1997), but the underlying methodologies used to derive the headcounts differ in important ways.

2. Anderson and Witter (1994, 21) argue that national income has traditionally been highly unequally distributed, reflecting the extreme disparities in the distribution of property.

3. Jamaican enjoyed rapid GDP growth of 6.3 per cent annually between 1952 and 1972, spurred by the development of bauxite mining and tourism (World Bank 2003, 1). Gordon (1987, 30–32) argues that Jamaicans whose parents were agricultural labourers, small farmers, domestics and unskilled manual workers had virtually no chance of ending up at the top of the middle class strata despite the expansion of the educational system. The inequality of opportunities is less sharp, though the gap between the middle strata, as a whole, and the mass of working class remains large, with the children of agricultural labourers and small farmers having the worst overall chance of upward mobility. However, individuals from the middle strata were also more likely to remain in this very strata.

4. Households are units, the members of which eat and dwell together as a rule; normally these persons maintain a common domestic economy, occupy a common dwelling, share common productive resources and liabilities, but this need not always be the case (Smith 1962).

5. Estimates for other towns and rural areas were derived by adjusting the cost of the KMA basket in keeping with relative prices in these regions (Osei 2002).

6. The resulting food basket was revised in 1995 after it was criticized as being too generous, especially in the sense of containing "relatively expensive foods from animal sources" (World Bank 1994). Revisions were also motivated by Ministry of Health concerns about the effect of the removal of subsidies on

households (PIOJ/STATIN 1997). The Pan American Health Organization and World Health Organization nutritional requirements were also revised downwards from 11,700 to 11,225 kilocalories per day for the representative family of five. The resulting food basket is referred to as the food poverty line and is the lower boundary of all poverty lines that are set.

7. For the purpose of this study adjustment for changes in price has been accounted for by the average consumer price index and uses a multiplier that is based on the consumption pattern of households in quintiles two, three and four. This is consistent with the recommendations of a review of the PIOJ method (Henry-Lee, Benfield and Ricketts 2000). The alternative poverty lines and headcount indices are shown in tables 2.1 and 2.2 respectively.

8. The multiplier approach is appealing since it reduces the number of budget categories for which explicit decisions must be made.

9. The official estimates of poverty are computed based on food shares for 1990.

10. This may be influenced by the underlying pattern of discrimination and preferences within the household. And changes in income and relative prices may affect estimated scales (Banks, Blundell and Preston 1991).

11. Laderchi, Saith and Stewart (2003) claim that individual resource needs are influenced by both theoretical and practical issues. From a rights-based perspective, all individuals have the same rights, so from this perspective equivalence scales and economies of scales may not be seen as applicable. However, if these rights are related to outcomes or adopting a utility-based perspective, adjustments that take account of different individual characteristics, such as equivalence scales, are justified.

12. Engel, cited in Deaton (1997), defines welfare with reference to the proportion of expenditure spent on food and suggest that this will decline with improvement in welfare. Households with the same level of food share are deemed as equally well off. On the other hand Rothbarth's (cited in Deaton 1997) method suggests that two households are equally well off when they are able to consume the same proportion of adult goods, such as clothing, alcohol or tobacco.

13. The minimum nutritional requirements are based on the Pan American Health Organization and the World Health Organization recommended standard for the members of a representative reference family of five: male adult, female adult and three children of different ages. The official poverty estimates used caloric requirements for females that are 0.741 of the male's requirements. The percentages of male requirements for the children were as follows: 0.452 for a child between 1 and 3 years; 0.76 for an older child between 10 and 14 years; and 0.8266 for a child in the 15 to 17 age group. According to Citro and Michael (1995), these equivalence scales are not internally consistent because they are based only on the dietary needs of family members even

though economies of scale appear to be different for food and household level public goods, like housing.

Chapter 3

1. Households were also asked, "How satisfied are you with life in general?" The responses were as follows: dissatisfied (20.0 per cent), very dissatisfied (18.4 per cent), neither satisfied/dissatisfied (24.6 per cent), satisfied (31.5 per cent), very satisfied (2.6 per cent) or don't know (2.4 per cent). The response to this question was considered to be much broader than the concept of poverty and therefore was not used.
2. An outlier of J$65,200 was dropped from the data. This household in fact resides in the rural area, and the response is closely related to the household expenditure on food of J$60,290.80 dollars.
3. The regional means specified by single female heads were much less than the mean minimum survival requirements specified by male-headed households, varying from a high of 31 per cent in urban regions to 7.4 per cent in rural areas. The disparity in requirements is even greater if maximum requirements specified by households in urban areas are looked at. This result may be motivated in part by the greater reliance of single-female-headed households on various forms of income support mechanisms and not just earned income.
4. If the maximum is compared with households' per-adult equivalent food expenditure, 11.9 per cent of households are below this threshold.
5. Using an ordered probit model and variables used in chapter 4 (table 4.2), households who are satisfied or very satisfied with life are predicted.
6. However, there will be households above this point who still feel that they are poor and households below the mean who feel that they are not poor.

Chapter 4

1. Easterlin (1995) also identifies habit formation as a potential factor influencing household expectations – "living level norms" – and this is informed by the utility one attaches to their current income level which is also influenced by their past income.
2. A critical assumption of the ordered probit is that of parallel slopes. This means that the variable Number of Children will affect the likelihood of a household being very poor, exactly as it will affect the likelihood of the household being poor. If this assumption was invalid, it would have been necessary to use the

method of multinomial logit to estimate the model. The literature also cautions about treating an outcome as ordered when in fact it is not and vice versa, and the resulting bias or loss of efficiency that results, but this is not applicable here. Similarly, the conditional logit model is not applicable since the data do not consist of choice-specific attributes, but instead individual-specific characteristics (Greene 2000, 862).

3. The probabilities associated with the observed responses of the model are:

$$\Pr(T_i = 1) = \Phi(Z_1 - \beta_k' x_{ik})$$
$$\Pr(T_i = 2) = \Phi(Z_2 - \beta_k' x_{ik}) - \Phi(Z_1 - \beta_k' x_{ik})$$
$$\Pr(T_i = j) = \Phi(Z_{j+1} - \beta_k' x_{ik})$$
$$\Pr(T_i = J) = 1 - \Phi(Z_J - \beta_k' x_{ik})$$

where i is any household, and j is a response alternative, such that $P(T_n=J)$ is the probability that household n responded in manner J, and $\Phi(\ )$ is the standard normal cumulative distribution function.

4. An obvious question which may be asked is how the probabilities of the various outcomes, more specifically, inadequate consumption/income or poor class – change when the value of one of the variables influencing the outcome changes. For a continuous variable the probability density function of the normal distribution is given as: $\Phi'(x) = d\Phi(x)/dx$. Positive signs on the model parameters indicate a fall in the probability of inadequate consumption levels or poorer classes, or increased probabilities of consumption being more than adequate or belonging to a wealthier class, as the associated variables increases, while negative signs suggest the converse. The effect of a dummy variable should be assessed by comparing the probabilities that result when the dummy variable takes one value with the probabilities that are the consequence of it taking the other value, ceteris paribus.

5. The multinomial logit model, though it could be used, will fail to account for the ordinal nature of the dependent variable and will not employ all of the information available in the variable. It is thus not used.

6. Jamaica is a relatively small country with a population of approximately 2.6 million (PIOJ 2008).

7. Of the total sample, these households represent 16.7 per cent, 17.0 per cent and 15.7 per cent for 1999, 1997, and 1993, respectively.

8. This is, however, different from the result in 1993 in which an average of 98.8 per cent of the estimated poor self-classified themselves as experiencing inadequate food consumption.

9. This is consistent with Chambers's (1994b, 1254) notion of seeking diversity, in which exceptions, oddities, dissenters and outliers are analysed.

10. When the higher level of economies of scale is applied, the proportion of households identified as unequivocally poor is reduced, possibly due to a reordering of households in the objective ranking.

Chapter 5

1. The obvious advantage of the pooled model is that it utilizes the information on the distribution of expenditure in its entirety (Grootaert 1997). This limitation of the levels regression was, however, dealt with by estimating separate functions for the poor. In addition, the levels regressions, according to Ravallion (1996a), can be estimated consistently under weaker assumptions about the distribution of the error. It is important to note that interest is not in whether the coefficients estimated over one group of the data (objective poor) are equal to the coefficient estimated over another (subjective poor), which can be done using the chow test. This is particularly the case since the groups are not mutually exclusive.

2. While it is possible to estimate a linear regression with a dichotomous dependent variable, the disturbances are heteroscedastic, and the model is likely to produce both nonsense probabilities and negative variances (Greene 2000, 813).

3. Most of these female heads (71.4 per cent) never married, while an average of 24.0 per cent are widowed.

4. Louat, Grosh and van der Gaag (1993), using the 1989 JSLC data, also show that the genders of the head of household and the student are significant determinants of enrolment. Although not taken up in this work, there is the possible effect of children's and their parents' expectation for employment on enrolment, resulting in little incentive to stay at school, which is sometimes overlooked.

5. The average number of days of attendance at school for all school age children within the household was computed.

6. Services for the disabled are provided mainly by the public sector and are aimed at integrating persons with disabilities into the economic and social life of Jamaica. In recent times, quotas have been used for the employment of disabled persons in the public sector and amendments to the building codes have been made to accommodate persons with disabilities. In addition, there are several initiatives planned in collaboration with the United States Agency for International Development that target persons with disabilities.

7. Approximately 95 per cent of the sample in 1999 had only one job.

8. This does not suggest a direction of causality and, in fact, higher consumption levels may have improved the ability of households to own these assets.

Chapter 6

1. Decomposition based on employer records by Hotchkiss and Moore (1996) suggests that 94 per cent of the predicted difference in salaries between men and women cannot be explained by differences in individual characteristics. They recognize that by not controlling for education, however, they may in fact have overestimated the portion of the differential that is unexplained. They also suggest that a substantial part of the differential is attributed to the fact that women tend to be employed in smaller firms and receive smaller rewards as firm size increases.

2. It is important to recognize that the category single-female-headed households lumps together categories of households generated by different processes at different life cycle stages and for different reasons, which are likely to have a variety of socio-economic circumstances and opportunities; any recommendation relating to single-female-headed households or comparison between male-headed households and single-female-headed households must therefore proceed cautiously (Whitehead and Lockwood 2003).

3. This is, however, somewhat different from findings for the United States, where women, although earning significantly less than males, are likely to report higher levels of job satisfaction.

4. Hotchkiss and Moore (1996) suggest that, while at every age, men employed in the government sector earn considerably more than women, both men and women employed in the government sector earn less than those in the private sector, with private sector earnings surpassing government sector earnings at age 22 and 26 for men and women respectively.

5. In such a case, the conventional consumption-based measure of welfare, which ignores leisure, will overstate the well-being of such vulnerable groups, with consequences for targeting and other policy interventions.

6. No literature on industrial segregation in Jamaica and its influence on earnings seems to be available.

7. The Duncan index measures the extent of difference in the distribution of males and females across occupational groups. The score varies between 0 and 100 and indicates the percentage of males (or females) that have to change their occupation in order for the distribution of both to be the same. A score of 0 indicates no segregation, while a score of 100 suggests complete segregation. Concern is raised about the use of highly aggregated occupational

classifications, in the case of Jamaica, to measure occupational segregation by gender and that generally, as the level of aggregation decreases, there is an accompanying increase in occupational segregation.

8. The *Economic and Social Survey of Jamaica* (PIOJ 2001) also suggests that of all landholders, less than one-third are women. Women also have less access to productive resources such as credit and participation in agricultural extension training programmes. Women are also underrepresented in parliament, local government, trade unions and the legal system. In addition, they are less likely to be recipients of national honours and awards.

9. Loutat et al. (1993), using the 1989 JSLC data, also show that the genders of the head of household and the student are significant determinants of enrolment. Although not taken up in this work, there is the possible effect of children's and their parents' expectations for employment on enrolment, resulting in little incentive to stay at school. This is sometimes overlooked.

10. Ennew and Young (1981) argue that dropping out of school usually happens when a student is between 10 and 12 years of age, particularly in the case of boys who fail the secondary school entrance examination and are big enough to generate a reasonable income by street vending, begging and pilfering as well as working in petty service industries. Here there is also the issue of truancy, for which there is little or no provision, possibly motivated by insufficient educational resources to provide for the number of children entitled to schooling, even under a shift system. Clearly, the issue of children's rights to education must not be overlooked.

11. The involvement of children in economic activities at the expense of their education is likely to perpetuate the intergenerational cycle of poverty, since they are likely to face higher time-rates of unemployment, lower income and a necessary involvement of the next generation of children in activities to supplement their parents' income.

12. The educational system requires both qualitative improvement and quantitative expansion if poor children, who are at the margins of both access and achievement, are to benefit. And the performance and attendance levels of boys are of major concern.

13. While the survey collects data on school attendance of children at school, no information on the activities of the out-of-school population is collected.

14. The average number of elderly and the dependency ratio in the sample is no different for single-female-headed households. However, relative to households correctly classified as poor, the average number of elderly and the dependency ratio is significantly less than in households incorrectly classified as poor.

15. There is no indication of the health status of the elderly in poor compared to non-poor households and its impact on their retirement decision, though Handa and Neitzert (1998) note that in the age group 45–65, Jamaican women report a higher incidence of chronic disease than for men. The elderly in non-poor households may no longer be employable or choose not to continue working since they do not need to. At the same time, loss of welfare may motivate non-poor households to incorrectly classify themselves as poor.

16. According to Kotlikoff and Spivak (1981, 388–89), the intergenerational consumption transfer and savings within families may, in part, be seen as a substitute for imperfect capital and annuity markets and is a method of smoothing consumption over time, whereby bequests and the ownership of assets are used as leverage and, if ignored, may not truly reflect the direction of resource transfer. The data, however, do not permit the extent and level of bequest to be established.

17. This intergenerational link is consistent with findings of Emerson and Souza (2003) for Brazil.

18. It may be too early to assess the impact of the PATH, which was first piloted in 2002.

19. If the argument that women are more altruistic towards children is accepted, then the positive effect of single-female-headed households on child labour possibly supports the conclusion that their vulnerability is not picked up by the household consumption data, but the literature on the direction of influence of female headship on child labour is not conclusive.

20. Primary education in the public system is free. The average cost of tuition and fees at the secondary level in 1999 was J$4,970, while the mean annual expenditure on other education-related items by households in 1999 was J$27,119. If the amount spent by households is seen as an indication of the requirements, clearly, it is prohibitive for many households.

21. However, Heady (2003), using data for Ghana and evidence from Pakistan and Nicaragua (Rosati and Rossi 2001), suggests that working does affect school performance.

22. Is fertility influenced by education or women's decision to work or does it, rather, depend on other exogenous influences or unobserved variables, such as preferences, operating on the basic sequence of lifetime choices (Schultz 1989, 5)?

23. Deepa et al. (2000) argue that many places where poor people live present multiple disadvantages such as missing and inadequate infrastructure and services, unfavourable geography, vulnerability to environmental shocks and seasonal exposure. Often these disadvantages combine in ways that endanger or impoverish those who live there.

24. However, using data for 1989, Psacharopoulos and Chu Ng (1992) suggest that females enjoyed a rate of return on schooling of 31.7 per cent compared to 28.0 per cent for males. This is possibly the reason why females outnumber males in all tertiary institutions in Jamaica.

Chapter 7

1. The multinomial logit model estimates the effects of explanatory variables on the dependent variable which have unordered response categories. The equation:

$$\text{Prob}\,(y = j) = \frac{e^{\sum_{k=1}^{K} \beta_{jk} x_k}}{1 + \sum_{j=1}^{J-1} e^{\sum_{k=1}^{K} \beta_{jk} x_k}}$$

gives Prob $(y = j)$ where $j = 1, 2, \dots J{-}1$. In the models $J = 1, 2$ and 3 are the incorrectly poor, non-poor and incorrectly not poor, and the base category is the unanimously poor. The parameter b has two subscripts, k for distinguishing x variables and j for distinguishing response categories.

2. This is compounded by the fact that many of these children may be attending schools of poorer quality.

3. Ennew and Young (1981) give an account of children who received no or only sporadic recompense for their labour, and they suggest that such exploitation may be compounded by the fact that the rates may be inadequate for the tasks performed.

4. For the period under review, unanimously poor households generally occupied two rooms, compared with between three and five rooms occupied by poor households incorrectly classified as not poor. Among the latter group, single-female-headed households generally occupied five rooms. This clearly shows that the use of the number of rooms as a targeting mechanism increases the likelihood of large type one error, excluding some of the poorest households.

5. However, it must be noted that females in the labour force generally possess higher levels of education than males. Women far outnumber men in academic and vocational success.

6. These findings support the fact that individuals' perceptions of their well-being are influenced by the social context, not only in terms of its influence on expectations, but also through strategic interactions.

7. There is also the unsubstantiated notion that females may have children by several males who they perceive can be of financial support, so, in some cases, all the siblings of a women may have different fathers.

8. This oversight in the conventional consumption measure of welfare is crucial when identifying the poor if, due to labour market distortions or other institutional factors, members of vulnerable groups must work longer hours to sustain the same level of consumption (Handa 1998).

9. If households made these decisions randomly, the fact that the amounts were not observed in all cases can be ignored and ordinary least squares regression used to estimate the model.

10. In the 1999 data, however, there were 94, 114 and 153 missing cases respectively, which include the average of those reporting receipt but not stating the amounts. Predictions were made for all missing cases, but it was only in cases where the household reported receipt of remittances that an amount was assigned.

11. This result is consistent with Adams and Page's (2003) findings that international remittances have a strong statistical impact on reducing poverty. They argue that a 10.0 per cent increase in the share of remittances in a country's GDP will lead to a 1.6 per cent decline in the share of people living on less than one US dollar per day.

References

Adams, R., and J. Page. 2003. *International migration, remittances and poverty in developing countries.* Policy Research Working Paper, no. 3179. Washington, DC: World Bank.

Anderson, P., and M. Witter. 1994. Crisis adjustment and social change: A case study of Jamaica. In *Consequences of structural adjustment: A review of the Jamaican experience,* ed. E. LeFranc, 1–55. Kingston: The Press, University of the West Indies.

Anker, R. 1997. Theories of occupational segregation by sex: An overview. *International Labour Review* 136 (3): 315–40.

Appleton, S. 1995. *"The rich are just like us only richer": Poverty functions or consumption functions.* London: Centre for the Study of African Economies, Oxford.

Atkinson, A.B. 1995. On targeting social security: Theory and Western experience with family benefits. In *Public spending and the poor: Theory and evidence,* ed. D. van de Walle and K. Need, 25–68. Baltimore: Johns Hopkins University Press.

Bailey, B. 2003. Gender-sensitive educational policy and practice: The case of Jamaica. Background paper for Education for All Global Monitoring Report, United Nations.

Bailey, B., and H. Ricketts. 2003. Gender vulnerabilities in Caribbean labour markets and decent work provisions. *Social and Economic Studies* 52 (4): 49–81.

Baland, J., and J. Robinson. 1998. *A model of child labour.* Working Paper, no. 206. Namur, Belgium: Centre de Recherche en Economie du Developpement, Facultes Universitaires, Notre-Dame de la Paix.

Banks, J., and P. Johnson. 1994. Equivalence scales and public policy. *Fiscal Studies* 15 (1): 1–23.

Banks, J., Blundell and I. Preston. 1991. Adult equivalent scales: A life-cycle perspective. *Fiscal Studies* 12 (13): 16–29.

Basu, K., and Z. Tzannatos. 2003. The global child labour problem: What do we know and what can we do? *World Bank Economic Review* 17 (2): 147–73.

Baulch, B., and J. Hoddinott. 2000. Economic mobility and poverty dynamics in developing countries. *Journal of Development Studies* 36 (6): 1–24.

Beckford, G.L. 1999. *Persistent poverty: Underdevelopment in plantation economies of the third world*. Kingston: University of the West Indies Press.

Behrman, J.R., and A.B. Deolaikar. 1990. *The poor and the social sector during a period of macroeconomic adjustment: Empirical evidence from Jamaica*. Working Paper, no. 152. Williamstown, MA: Department of Economics, Williams College.

Benfield, W. 2007. Optimum targeting: The Jamaica food stamp programme. *Journal of Social and Economic Studies* 56 (4): 121–64.

Besley, T., and R. Kanbur. 1993. The principles of targeting. In *Including the poor*, ed. M. Lipton and J. Van der Gaag, 67–90. Washington, DC: World Bank.

Bevan, P., and S.F. Joireman. 1997. The perils of measuring poverty: Identifying the poor in rural Ethiopia. *Oxford Development Studies* 25 (3): 315–43.

Bhalotra, S. 2003. Child labour in Asia and Africa. Background research paper for the Education For All Monitoring Report, University of Bristol.

Bhalotra, S., and C. Heady. 2003. Child farm labor: The wealth paradox. *World Bank Economic Review* 17 (2): 197–227.

Bhalotra, S., and Z. Tzannatos. 2002. *Child labour: What have we learnt?* Social Protection Discussion Paper, no. 317. Washington, DC: World Bank.

Blanchflower, D., and A. Oswald. 2004. Well-being over time in Britain and the USA. *Journal of Public Economics* 88 (7–8): 1359–87.

Booth, D., J. Holland, J. Hentschel, P. Lanjouw and A. Herbert. 1998. *Participation and combining methods in Africa poverty assessment: Renewing the agenda*. London: Department for International Development.

Boyd, D.A.C. 1988. *Economic management, income distribution, and poverty in Jamaica*. London: Praeger.

Carletto, G., and A. Zezza. 2004. Being poor, feeling poorer: Combining objective and subjective measures of welfare in Albania. *Journal of Development Studies* 42 (5): 739–60.

Carvalho, S., and H. White. 1997. *Combining the quantitative and qualitative approaches of poverty measurement and analysis: The practice and the potential*. World Bank Technical Paper, no. 366. Washington, DC: World Bank.

Castilla, C. 2009. *Objective versus subjective poverty: Are income positional concerns influencing subjective poverty assessments?* Working Paper Series. Columbus: Ohio State University, Department of Agricultural, Environmental and Development Economics.

Castle, S. 1995. Child fostering and children's nutritional outcomes in Mali: The role of female status in directing child transfer. *Social Science and Medical Journal* 40 (5): 679–93.

Chambers, R. 1994a. The origins and practice of participatory rural appraisal. *World Development* 22 (7): 953–69.

———. 1994b. Participatory rural appraisal (PRA): Analysis of experiences. *World Development* 22 (9): 1253–68.

———. 1997. *Whose reality counts? Putting the first last.* London: Intermediate Technology Publications.

Citro, C.F., and R.T. Michael, eds. 1995. *Measuring poverty: A new approach.* Washington, DC: National Academy Press.

Clark, A.E., and A.J. Oswald. 1994. Unhappiness and unemployment. *Economic Journal* (104): 648–59.

Deaton, A. 1997. *The analysis of household surveys: A microeconomic approach to development policy.* Baltimore: Johns Hopkins University Press.

Deepa, N., R. Chambers, K.S. Meera and P. Patti, eds. 2000. *Voices of the poor: Crying out for change.* New York: Oxford University Press.

Desai, M., and A. Shah. 1988. An econometric approach to the measurement of poverty. *Oxford Economic Papers* 40 (3): 505–22.

Desgupta, P. 1996. *An inquiry into well-being and destitution.* New York: Oxford University Press.

Di Tella, R., R. MacCulloch and A. Oswald. 2003. The macroeconomics of happiness. *Review of Economics and Statistics* 85 (4): 809–27.

Dollar, D., and A. Kraay. 2000. *Growth is good for the poor.* Policy Research Working Paper, no. 2587. Washington, DC: World Bank.

Easterlin, R. 1995. Will raising the incomes of all increase the happiness of all? *Journal of Economic Behaviour and Organisation* 27 (1): 35–47.

Emerson, P.M., and A.P. Souza. 2003 Is there a child labor trap? Intergenerational persistence of child labor in Brazil. *Economic Development and Cultural Change* 51 (2): 375–98.

Ennew, J., and P. Young. 1981. Child labour in Jamaica. *Child Labour Series* 6. London: Anti-Slavery Society.

Ferguson, J. 1992. Jamaica: Stories of poverty. *Race and Class* 34 (1): 61–72.

Foster, J., J. Greer and E. Thorbecke. 1984. A class of decomposable poverty measures. *Econometrica* 52 (3): 761–66.

Frijters, P., J.P. Haisken-DeNew and M.A. Shields. 2004. Investigating the patterns and determinants of life satisfaction in Germany following reunification. *Journal of Human Resources* 39 (3): 649–74.

Gordon, D. 1987. Class, status and social mobility in Jamaica. Kingston: Institute for Social and Economic Research, University of the West Indies.

Greeley, M. 1994. Measurement of poverty and poverty of measurement. *IDS Bulletin* 25 (2): 50–58.

Greene, W. 2000. *Econometric analysis.* 4th ed. New York: Macmillan.

Grootaert, C. 1997. The determinants of poverty in Cote d'Ivoire in the 1980s. *Journal of African Economies* 6 (2): 169–96.

———. 1998. *Child labour in Cote d'Ivoire: Incidence and determinants.* Washington, DC: World Bank.

Grootaert, C. and R. Kanbur. 1995. Child labour: An economic perspective. *International Labour Review* 134 (2): 187–203.

Grootaert, C., R. Kanbur and G. Oh. 1997. The dynamics of welfare gains and losses: An African case study. *Journal of Development Studies* 33 (5): 635–57.

Haddad, L., and R. Kanbur. 1991. Upper-limit indicator targeting and age-based nutritional interventions: Optimality, information and leakage. Discussion Paper, no. 107, University of Warwick.

Handa, S. 1998. Are female-headed households time poor? Evidence from Jamaica. *Social and Economic Studies* 47 (4): 1–27.

Handa, S., and M. Neitzert. 1998. *Chronic illness and retirement in Jamaica.* World Bank Living Standards Measurement Study Working Paper, no. 131. Washington, DC: World Bank.

Heady, C. 2003. The effect of child labor on learning achievement. *World Development* 31 (2): 385–98.

Henry-Lee, A., W. Benfield and H. Ricketts. 2000. Reviewing the current methodology used in formulating and calculating the poverty line. Planning Institute of Jamaica, symposium on poverty, September 2000.

Honig, B. 1996. Educational and self-employment in Jamaica. *Comparative Educational Review* 40 (2): 177–93.

Hotchkiss, J., and R. Moore. 1996. Gender compensation differentials in Jamaica. *Economic Development and Cultural Change* 44 (3): 657–76.

Jalan, J., and M. Ravallion. 2000. Is transient poverty different? Evidence for rural China. *Journal of Development Studies* 36 (6): 82–99.

James, V., and C. Williams. 2004. Financing higher education: Policy choices for Jamaica. Paper presented at Mona Academic Conference on the Future of Higher Education in Jamaica, University of the West Indies, Kingston.

Jodha, N.S. 1988. Poverty debate in India: A minority view. *Economic and Political Weekly* 23 (45–47): 2421–28.

Johnson, H.G. 1966. Unemployment and poverty: Unemployment, underemployment, fiscal and monetary policy, economic policy. *Asia Pacific Journal of Human Resources* 1 (6): 127–28.

Kassouf, A.L. 1998. Child labour in Brazil. Typescript. London School of Economics and University of Sao Paulo.

Kilpatrick, R.W. 1973. The income elasticity of the poverty line. *Review of Economics and Statistics* 55 (3): 327–32.

Kotlikoff, L.J., and A. Spivak. 1981. The family as an incomplete annuities market. *Journal of Political Economy* 89 (2): 372–91.

Krishna, A. 2004. Escaping poverty and becoming poor: Who gains, who loses, and why? *World Development* 32 (1): 121–36.

Laderchi, C.R. 1997. Poverty and its many dimensions: The role of income as an indicator. *Oxford Development Studies* 25 (3): 345–60.

Laderchi, C., R. Saith and F. Stewart. 2003. *Does it matter that we don't agree on the definition of poverty? A comparison of four approaches.* University of Oxford Working Paper, no. 107, Queen Elizabeth House, Oxford University.

Lipton, M., and M. Ravallion. 1995. Poverty and policy. In *Handbook of development economics.* 1st ed., vol. 3, ed. H. Chenery and T.N. Srinivasan, 2551–57. Amsterdam: Elsevier.

Lok-Dessallien, R. 2000. Review of poverty concepts and indicators. New York: UNDP. Available from: http.//www.undp.org/poverty/publications/pov-red/poverty-assessments.pdf

Lokshin, M., and M. Ravallion. 2002. *Rich and powerful? Subjective power and welfare in Russia.* Policy Research Working Paper, no. 2854. Washington, DC: World Bank.

Louat, F., M. Grosh and J. van der Gaag. 1993. *Welfare implications of female headship in Jamaica households.* Living Standards Measurement Study Working Paper, no. 96. Washington, DC: World Bank.

Lundberg, M.K.A., and P.K. Diskin. 1995. Targeting assistance to the poor and food insecure: A literature review. Technical Paper no. 9, Office of Sustainable Development, Bureau for Africa, USAID.

McCulloch, N., and B. Baulch. 2000. Simulating the impact of policy upon chronic and transitory poverty in rural Pakistan. *Journal of Development Studies* 36 (6): 100–130.

McCulloch, N., and M. Calandrino. 2002. *Poverty dynamics in rural Sichuan between 1991 and 1995.* IDS Working Papers, no. 151. Brighton: Institute of Development Studies.

Mehrotra, S. 2000. Social development in high-achieving countries: Common elements and diversities. In *Development with a human face: Experience in social achievement and economic growth*, ed. S. Mehrotra and R. Jolly, 21–61. New York: Oxford University Press.

Moser, C., and J. Holland. 1997. *Urban poverty and violence in Jamaica*. Washington, DC: World Bank.

Mukherjee, S., and T. Benson. 2003. The determinants of poverty in Malawi, 1998. *World Development* 31 (2): 339–58.

Olsen, R., and A. Coppin. 2001. The determinants of gender differences in income in Trinidad and Tobago. *Journal of Development Studies* 37 (5): 31–56.

Orshansky, M. 1965. Counting the poor: Another look at the poverty profile. *Social Security Bulletin* 28 (1): 3–29.

Osei, P. 2002. A critical assessment of the Jamaica's national poverty eradication programme. *Journal of International Development* 14 (6): 773–88.

Pal, S. 2004. How much of the gender difference in child school enrolment can be explained? Evidence from rural India. *Bulletin of Economic Research* 56 (2): 133–58.

Planning Institute of Jamaica (PIOJ). 2000. *Jamaica Human Development Report 2000*. Kingston: PIOJ.

———. 2001. *Economic and Social Survey Jamaica 2000*. Kingston: PIOJ.

———. 2008. *Economic and Social Survey Jamaica 2000*. Kingston: PIOJ.

Planning Institute of Jamaica and Statistical Institute of Jamaica (STATIN). 1996. *Jamaica Survey of Living Conditions Report, 1995*. Kingston: PIOJ.

———. 2000. *Jamaica Survey of Living Conditions Report, 1999*. Kingston: PIOJ.

———. 2001. *Jamaica Survey of Living Conditions Report, 2000*. Kingston: PIOJ.

Pradhan, M., and M. Ravallion. 2000. Measuring poverty using qualitative perceptions of consumption adequacy. *Review of Economics and Statistics* (82): 462–71.

Preston, J. 1999. Occupational gender segregation: Trends and explanations. *Quarterly Review of Economics and Finance* 39 (5): 611–24.

Psacharopoulos, G. 1997. Child labor versus educational attainment: Some evidence from Latin America. *Journal of Population Economics* 10 (4): 1–10.

Psacharopoulos, G., and Ying Chu Ng. 1992. *Earnings and education in Latin America: Assessing priorities for schooling investment*. Working Paper, no. 1056. Washington, DC: World Bank.

Pyatt, G. 2003. Poverty versus the poor. In *The new poverty strategies. What have they achieved? What have we learned?*, ed. A. Booth and P. Mosley, 91–119. New York: Palgrave Macmillan.

Quentin, W. 2007. Is there a divergence between objective measures and subjective perceptions of poverty trends? Evidence from West and Central Africa. MPRA Paper 10486, University Library of Munich.

Ravallion, M. 1992. *Poverty comparisons: A guide to concepts and methods.* Living Standards Measuring Study Working Paper, no. 88. Washington, DC: World Bank.

———. 1996. Issues in measuring and modelling poverty. *Economic Journal* (106): 1328–43.

———. 1998. *Poverty lines in theory and practice.* Living Standards Measurement Study Working Paper 133. Washington, DC: World Bank.

Ravallion, M., and B. Bidani. 1994. How robust is poverty profile? *World Bank Economic Review* 8 (1): 75–102.

Ravallion, M., and M. Lokshin. 1999. *Subjective economic welfare.* Policy Research Working Paper, no. 2106. Washington, DC: World Bank.

———. 2000. *Identifying welfare effects from subjective questions.* Policy Research Working Paper, no. 2301. Washington, DC: World Bank.

Ravallion, M., and Q. Wodon. 2000. Does child labour displace schooling? Evidence on behavioural response to an enrolment subsidy. *Economic Journal* 110 (462): 158–75.

Ray, R. 1999. *How child labour and child schooling interact with adult labour?* Policy Research Working Paper, no. 2179. Washington, DC: World Bank.

Ricketts, H. 2005. Dimensions of disadvantage and exclusion: Sociology and the wage determination process. Paper presented at the Ninth Annual Derek Gordon Seminar, University of the West Indies, Kingston.

Ricketts, H., and W. Benfield. 2000. Gender and the Jamaican labour market: The decade of the 90s. In *The construction of gender development indicators for Jamaica,* ed. P. Mohammed, 41–56. Kingston: PIOJ/UNDP/CIDA.

Robb, C.M. 1999. *Directions in development: Can the poor influence policy? Participatory poverty assessments in the developing world.* Washington, DC: World Bank.

Rosati, C.F., and M. Rossi. 2001. *Children's working hours, school enrolment and human capital accumulation: Evidence from Pakistan and Nicaragua.* Geneva: International Labour Organisation.

Rowntree, B.S. 1901. *Poverty: A study of town life.* London: Macmillan.

Sahn, D.E. 1999. None income dimensions of poverty: A note of research findings and issues. World Development Report Workshop on Poverty, World Bank, Washington, DC.

Satz, D. 2003. Child labour: A normative perspective. *World Bank Economic Review* 17 (2): 297–309.

Schultz, P.T. 1989. *Women and development: Objectives, frameworks, and policy interventions.* Policy Planning and Research Working Paper, no. 200. Washington, DC: World Bank.

Schumpeter, E.B., ed. 1994. *History of economic analysis: Joseph A. Schumpeter.* New York: Oxford University Press.

Scott, K. 1992 Female labour force participation and earnings: The case of Jamaica. In *Case studies on women's employment and pay in Latin America,* ed. G. Psacharopoulos and Z. Tzannatos, 323–38. Washington, DC: World Bank.

Smith, A. 1910. *The wealth of nations.* New York: Everyman's Library.

Smith, M.G. 1962. *West Indian family structure.* Seattle: University of Washington Press.

———. 1989. *Poverty in Jamaica.* Kingston: Institute of Social and Economic Research, University of the West Indies.

Stanovnik, T. 1992. Perception of poverty and income satisfaction. *Journal of Economic Psychology* 13 (21): 57–69.

Subrahmanian, R. 2004. Promoting gender equality. In *Targeting development: Critical perspectives on the Millennium Development Goals,* ed. R. Black and H. White, 384. London: Routledge.

Theodossiou, I. 1998. The effects of low-pay and unemployment on psychological well-being: A logistical regression approach. *Journal of Health Economics* 17 (1): 85–104.

Townsend, P. 1979. *Poverty in the United Kingdom: A survey of household resources and standard of living.* London: Penguin.

Van Praag, B.M.S., and A. Ferrer-i-Carbonell. 2008. A multi-dimensional approach to subjective poverty. In *Quantitative approaches to multi-dimensional poverty assessment,* ed. N. Kakwani and J. Silber, chapter 8. New York: Palgrave Macmillan.

Veenhoven, R. 2004. Subjective measures of well-being. WIDER Discussion Paper 2004/07. Helsinki: United Nations University–World Institute for Development Economics Research.

White, H. 2002. Combining quantitative and qualitative approaches in poverty analysis. *World Development* 30 (3): 511–22.

White, H., and E. Anderson. 2000. *Growth versus distribution: Does the pattern of growth matter?* Brighton: Institute of Development Studies.

White, H., and E. Masset. 2003. The importance of household size and composition in constructing poverty profiles: An illustration from Vietnam. *Development and Change* 34 (1): 105–26.

Whitehead, A., and M. Lockwood. 2003. Gendering poverty: A review of six World Bank African poverty assessments. In *The new poverty strategies: What have they achieved? What have we learned?*, ed. A. Booth and P. Mosley, 223–52. New York: Palgrave Macmillan.

World Bank. 1994. *Jamaica. A strategy for growth and poverty reduction: Country economic memorandum*. Washington, DC: World Bank.

———. 2000. *World development report 2000/2001: Attacking poverty*. New York: Oxford University Press.

———. 2003. *The road to sustained growth in Jamaica: World Bank country study*. Washington, DC: World Bank.

Index

www.ingramcontent.com/pod-product-compliance
Lightning Source LLC
Chambersburg PA
CBHW030651270326
41929CB00007B/304